Intellectual

Intellectual Pursuits

*Toward an
Understanding of Culture*

Bernard Barber

ROWMAN & LITTLEFIELD PUBLISHERS, INC.
Lanham • Boulder • New York • Oxford

ROWMAN & LITTLEFIELD PUBLISHERS, INC.

Published in the United States of America
by Rowman & Littlefield Publishers, Inc.
4720 Boston Way, Lanham, Maryland 20706
12 Hid's Copse Road
Cumnor Hill, Oxford OX2 9JJ, England

British Library Cataloguing in Publication Information Available

Library of Congress Cataloging-in-Publication Data

Barber, Bernard.
    Intellectual pursuits : toward an understanding of culture /
Bernard Barber.
        p.   cm.
    Includes bibliographical references and index.
    ISBN 0-8476-8859-3 (alk. paper).—ISBN 0-8476-8860-7 (pbk. :
alk. paper)
        1. Intellectuals.   2. Intellectual life.   3. Culture.   I. Title.
HM213.B334   1998
305.5'52—dc21   97-51883
                                                                CIP

ISBM 0-8476-8859-3 (cloth : alk. paper)
ISBN 0-8476-8860-7 (pbk. : alk. paper)

Printed in the United States of America

♾ ™ The paper used in this publication meets the minimum requirements of
American National Standard for Information Sciences—Permanence of Paper for
Printed Library Materials, ANSI Z39.48–1984.

For Bridget and Bob Lyons

the best of friends and intellectual companions

Contents

Acknowledgments

For many different kinds of encouragement and help, I thank Jeffrey Alexander, Dean Birkenkamp, Aida DiPace Donald, Alex Inkeles, Neil Smelser, Charles Tilly, and Viviana R. Zelizer. As always, I am especially indebted to Elinor G. Barber for moral, emotional, and intellectual help.

Introduction

This book deals with a set of highly interconnected theoretical and empirical research problems that has challenged my central concerns as a sociologist and sociological theorist over several decades. Hence the frequent references to my earlier work, to books and articles that contain essential but much less developed prototypes of the ideas offered here. The most important element of the references to my earlier work is manifest in my version of social system theory, which I have been developing and applying these many years to produce a more social scientific and, hopefully, helpful understanding of the topics of culture and intellectuals than presently exists.[1]

Since my analysis of culture and of "intellectual pursuits" in this book is often quite different from most of that in the existing multitudinous writings on those topics, it would seem helpful to make two general features of this book explicit. The first is that it intends, indeed, to be social scientific, and therefore rejects the assumption, now held by a great many of my colleagues in sociology, in the social sciences, and the humanities more generally, that objective, nonrelativistic social science is impossible.

The second and related general feature of the book is that it intends to insist, positively, on the effectiveness of its particular systematic analysis, rather than to explicate the mixture of defects, limitations, and virtues of the corps of relativist theorists who have so much influ-

---

1. For a full statement, see Bernard Barber, *Constructing the Social System* (New Brunswick, NJ, Transaction Books, 1993).

enced the social sciences and the humanities since the 1960s. This is not the place to present my views of such relativists as Geertz,[2] Foucault, Habermas, and Bourdieu, and the multitude of lesser lights who have followed them. I am sufficiently familiar with these writers and with powerful critiques of their work[3] to know very well that their view of social theory and social reality is not mine. Since all social science, however primarily objective, may secondarily have explicit or implicit significance for what I will define in chapter 3 as ideology, then I repeat, this book intends to be wholly scientific, not ideological, although it might be used by others, secondarily, as an ideology for science in general and social science specifically. As we shall see, ideologies may be based in fact; they become ideologies only when the facts are used to justify or criticize some value, norm, or value-derived policy preference.

In addition to explaining these two general features of the book, I would like to lay out the purposes, substances, and interrelations among the five chapters that make up the body of the book. Brief descriptions foreshadow the several interconnected detailed discussions that are essential for a fuller understanding of the two complex topics of culture and intellectual pursuits. They will make it clear that this book has no simple, single message or thesis; it does not have a capsule definition of either "intellectuals" or "culture." Indeed, I shall emphasize in the discussions of the two topics of what will be called "intellectual pursuits" and "culture" how the analyses of these two topics enrich each other. The several parts of the book are intended to provide a better understanding of the complexity and interrelations among the various aspects of these central concerns.

---

2. For example, I have been a close student of the work of Clifford Geertz over the last forty years. His earlier work on Indonesia, Morocco, and Islam I considered outstanding objective social science. But although I have continued to read his work right up to the present, still, since about twenty years ago, when he began to use subjective, relativist ideas such as "blurred genres" and "thick description," I have come to deplore and regret his falling away from objective, cumulative social science.

3. For some especially admirable examples of such critiques, see Jeffrey Alexander, "Habermas' New Critical Theory: Its Promise and Problems," *American Journal of Sociology*, 91 (1985): 400–24; and "The Reality of Reduction: The Failed Synthesis of Pierre Bourdieu" in Alexander, *Fin-de-Siecle Social Theory* (London, Verso 1995), 128–217.

Chapter 1 is the more concrete prelude to the more systematic analysis of intellectuals and culture in the following chapters; it is a screen off which the positive and complex definitions of intellectuals and culture in those chapters can be highlighted. By looking closely at the writings of a diverse group of able people who call themselves intellectuals, who are also so named by others, or who write about intellectuals, chapter 1 attempts a vivid demonstration of how the use of the term "intellectual" is vague, variable, and inconsistent. This chapter makes it clear that the term "intellectual" is greatly in need of clarification. It suggests that there are many different kinds of intellectual functions that need to be specified. Indeed, because there are so many different intellectual functions, I have decided to write about intellectual pursuits rather than about intellectuals. By the use of the term, "intellectual pursuits" it is possible to say useful things not only about intellectual activities in general, as in the discussion of intellectual structure in chapter 4 on the problem of "high" and "low" forms of culture, but also intensively to analyze each of the many differentiated kinds of intellectual pursuit, as I do for ideology, in chapter 3. As a matter of fact, many of the writers examined in chapter 1 are indeed primarily ideologists, and their work can be better understood in the light of this later comprehensive discussion of ideology. Since social systems cannot operate without a variety of intellectuals, it will be useful for the more effective functioning of social systems if these diverse roles, and some of the problems that result for these roles, are well understood, again both by the different types of intellectuals themselves and by other kinds of actors in their societies. An example of such resulting problems is taken up in chapter 5.

Chapter 2 takes up a positive and comprehensive analysis of culture and intellectual pursuits. Its point is that a systematic theory of culture derived from social system theory is essential for clarifying and specifying the diverse types of intellectual pursuits. Culture, in that theory, is defined as being about meanings, expressed in ideas and other kinds of symbols, and that is surely also what intellectuals of all kinds are concerned about. Ideas and symbols are the bedrock of intellectual pursuits; that is the bedrock of agreement in discussions about intellectuals.

Of course, "culture" itself has too often become a vague concept,[4] but social system theory offers a precise general definition and an extensive list of the many special functional types of ideas and symbols that make up the culture system as a whole. With this theory of culture it is possible to sort out the different kinds of intellectual pursuits and clarify the relations among them, both the harmonious relations and those that present tensions and problems. The last chapter, for example, will discuss the cultural tensions and conflicts that often occur among scholars and scientists, on the one hand, and ideologists and social reformers with a variety of value agendas, on the other, all of these latter often lumped together undifferentiatedly as intellectuals.

Chapter 3 provides an intensive analysis of one important component of culture and one kind of intellectual pursuit. It seeks primarily to rescue the term "ideology" for objective social science and, secondarily, to show that very frequently the term "intellectuals" is used synonymously with what should more specifically and accurately be called ideologists. All social systems operate with a variety of values and norms and it is the essential function of certain intellectuals as ideologists to make more or less simple, more or less complex, justifying and criticizing statements about the values and norms that societies and their sub-systems have chosen. That is what ideology basically is: a statement justifying or criticizing some value or norm. Some intellectuals in the role of ideologists also justify and criticize the policy options and decisions that governments and other social organizations make to realize the values and norms that are either explicitly or implicitly to be achieved in proposed or actual policy decisions. Because of the value choices that are endemic to social systems, they are endlessly faced with policy decisions and with their associated justifying and criticizing ideologies of all kinds.

Though important everywhere, the ideological function is itself differently valued in different societies and at different times in the same society. Thus, in Marxist Russia, ideologist was an established and prestigious occupational role. In American society, partly in reaction against Marxist approval of the term and its actual use in the Soviet

---

4. Once again, I repeat that it is not my purpose here to review in detail the large, frequently unsatisfactory literature on culture.

system, but also because of our rationalist bent, ideologists are not called by that name, but they nevertheless follow the same intellectual pursuit under currently more socially acceptable rubrics, favorable and unfavorable, such as public intellectuals, public relations experts, newspaper columnists, spin doctors, and many others. Nowhere, as Professor Tony Judt has very convincingly argued, are intellectuals as ideologists more visible, more centralized (in Paris), and more prestigious than in France.

Chapter 4 moves on to consider a general characteristic pertaining to all culture and all intellectual pursuits, namely, that there is always a structure to the symbols and meanings of that culture and those pursuits. This chapter takes up the perennial controversies over one aspect of that structure, which is whether cultural symbols manifest themselves in "higher" and "lower" forms, what the analytical dimensions of higher and lower are, and what the social processes are by which decisions are made in determining higher and lower forms. All intellectual functions—those of cognitively transmitting, normatively justifying and criticizing, and esthetically expressing the ideas and symbols of culture—occur not just at the high but at a variety of high, middle, and low cultural levels. While the elite intellectuals may be more visible, social systems are filled with street philosophers, everyday opinion-holders, and mass publication columnists who provide information and also articulate the value-justifying statements that result in an inevitable amount of conflict or integration between the elite and popular levels of the society.

We stress that the concept of high and low culture applies to all of culture's component functions: science and art as well as ideology and all the others, and therefore this chapter might well have come before the previous one on ideology. But it seems useful in the chapter on ideology to provide analysis and material on one cultural function that exemplifies the specific central message of this one.

In sum, this chapter seeks to give an answer to the difficult question of how we can objectively classify cultural products, verbal, musical, or symbolic, as high, middle, or low. There has been a lot of common-sense and ideological struggling with and controversy over this important problem. An objective and analytic solution is desirable.

Finally, chapter 5 looks at a case of a general phenomenon in social systems, tension and conflict between different kinds of intellectual pursuits. I have chosen the illustrative case of different kinds of intellectual pursuits ("cultural specialists" was the term used by Talcott Parsons) in the university, where it is often assumed that only objective scholarship prevails. Intellectuals in the academy often divide into scientists and scholars, on the one hand, and ideologists and reformers, on the other. This results in tension and conflict between them and even within them in some cases. That is, individual members of the academy sometimes do not stick to their principal or preferred role; scholars or scientists may become ideologists, often without knowing it. And ideologists may claim to be only objective scholars.

This may cause confusion and conflict both for the academic intellectuals themselves and for others in their society. However, as Judt points out about the intellectuals he studied in post-World War II France, the elite artists, such as Picasso (except perhaps for the Guernica painting), were able to separate their primary function as artists from their ideological function as ardent supporters of the French Communist Party. In contrast, lesser figures in science and the arts let their communist ideology overwhelm their presumably central role expertise.

One of the important problems today for the development of the social sciences is the existence among its practitioners of diverse intellectual aspirations: some want to be primarily scientists, others to be primarily ideologists and reformers. In many areas of the social sciences it is not always easy to discriminate the science from the ideology. As a result, the social sciences are often a mishmash of the two, and adherents of the two different functions quarrel bitterly with one another.

So much for these brief statements of the general and specific contents of the several chapters of this book, all to be expanded in the chapters themselves. A few qualifications are in order. It should now be clear that the primary purpose of the book is social scientific, to improve our theoretical understanding of culture and intellectual pursuits by the use of general social system theory. But this enterprise is not just a matter of abstract theoretical propositions. Comparative empirical illustration of the propositions is absolutely essential, as it almost always is for valid theoretical analysis. However, given the enormous mass of existing comparative empirical material, about all kinds of societies from earlier historical periods and quite different types of cultures, it is necessary to be quite selective from this superabundance. Wherever possible, material from different historical periods and societies will be cited, but exemplification leans heavily on American society and to contemporary examples. Note carefully, however, that the analysis is applicable in principle to all societies at all times. In practice, of course, as different societies and historical periods are studied, the analysis will need to be modified and amplified. Which is only to say that, like all scientific analysis, this one is provisional, hopefully the best that can be done at this time. And, hopefully also, it will have some practical significance and consequences, improving both general and expert intellectual discourse.

1

❧ ❧ ❧

What is an Intellectual?
A Brief Look at the Confusion

This chapter is a prelude to the systematic analysis of culture and intellectual pursuits presented in the four following chapters of this book. In contrast to that later positive analysis, we look here at some of the present confusion in prominent places about culture and intellectual pursuits. The purpose here is not *negative*; this is not a critique of the enormous amount of previous writing about culture and intellectuals.

Everyday language is filled with a considerable number of important words that have vague, diverse, even contradictory meanings in their common usage, terms like "love," "trust," "fashion," "community," "poverty," and "class," to name only a few. Of course, that language also has a great many precise, technically defined words. How could it be otherwise, if communication is to proceed, as it does, on the whole, relatively effectively? Physicists know how to use "atom" precisely, biologists to use "virus" similarly, and economists to use "money" or "market" more or less precisely. The man in the street uses terms like "home run" or "jump shot" with precision equal to the scientist speaking of "atoms." But both scientists and ordinary people also use a whole set of terms such as I have mentioned above with large and equal vagueness, diversity, and inconsistency.

One such word is "intellectual," used more often by educated people

1

than others, to be sure, but sometimes used slightingly by those among the less educated who pride themselves on their common sense and practicality to refer to those of the educated whom they consider impractical. In brief, it is one key purpose of this book to clarify the use of this term, to give it some precise and expanded meanings and contexts, to show how these diverse meanings and contexts are related to one another, and point the way to eliminating the confusion and tension that result from vagueness and diversity. To accomplish such clarification requires rejecting a simplistic, singular definition in favor of an examination of a number of different aspects of intellectual activity. That is why this book is called *Intellectual Pursuits: Towards an Understanding of Culture*; the title is designed to carry our understanding forward to the actually complex meanings and aspects of intellectual activities and the culture from which they are derived. Inevitably, this exercise will challenge common sense and meet with resistance; but that often occurs for many such exercises.

The Social Sciences and the Clarification of Terms

Our particular concern with the term "intellectual" is only one example of the general and essential concern that the social sciences have in using general social system theory to clarify vague everyday language.[1] To understand social life better, to make some improvement in it, we need more precise words and sentences. And where vagueness and diversity of usage in language seem hard to overcome, and even somewhat useful, we need to know why that is the case. As its own history shows, this essential task of social sciences has never been, and will continue not to be, an easy one. Many divergent values, many conflicting interests, and many strongly held ideas and emotions are deeply involved in the kind of terms of interest here. There is often widespread and strong resistance in popular and also specialist circles to new ideas, and especially to new terms to express those new ideas. Charges of "jargon" confront social science on all sides. As I have

---

1. For examples of the vagueness, diversity, and contradictoriness of sentences, see any collection of commonsense sayings and aphorisms.

elsewhere shown, there is even some "resistance by scientists to scientific discovery."[2] Originality and innovation in the world of culture, of ideas and symbols, are often hard-won.

One successful example of the expansion of a term by a social scientist is the work in the 1930s on what the sociological criminologist, Professor Edwin S. Sutherland of Indiana University, perhaps for the first time, called "white-collar crime." Until that time both popular and sociological discussions of crime limited it to the thefts and violence of lower-class criminals. Sutherland's book, combining theoretical analysis and empirical data, showed the great extent and special character of middle-class or white-collar crime. It is a phrase that has now gone into both the popular and the professional literature. It has had a considerable influence on legal and social policy. The notion of white-collar crime is now "common sense."

I have myself made two similar attempts to clarify and extend the meaning of some important commonsense terms, so far without any great success. One is the term "fashion," used everywhere in a loose way with regard to changes of style and focus in clothing, music, science, and just about every other sphere of cultural ideas and symbols. With data from the development of the sociology of medicine and from science in general, I have tried to show that the vague term "fashion" is always about social and cultural change and that any discussion of fashion, therefore, should specify different aspects of an alleged fashion: its social and cultural sources, its patterns, its rates of change, and its social and cultural consequences. No luck: multiple and frequent vague uses of the term "fashion" flourish.

My second effort has been to clarify and expand the meanings of what is an equally popular and vague word in both everyday and professional discourse, namely, "trust." I have argued, again on both theoretical and empirical grounds, that common usage of the idea of trust confuses two independently variable matters. One is trust as technically competent performance; thus, we trust that a physician can perform a thorough and satisfactory general health examination or

---

2. See my "Resistance by Scientists to Scientific Discovery," *Science* 134 (1961): 596–602. Apparently because resistance is widely experienced among scientists, many hundreds of scientists wrote for reprints of this article, and it has been widely cited and reprinted.

perform the particular procedure in which he claims to be a specialist, for example, by-pass surgery. The other aspect of trust is fiduciary responsibility: thus, we trust that a professional physician will put the interests of the patient before his own financial or career interests. Some of the current distrust of the medical profession does question their technically competent performance. But another, and perhaps currently more common, source of popular distrust is the belief that the medical profession puts its own interests before those of its patients. It is clear that performances in many fields may be technically competent without observing fiduciary responsibility.

And vice versa, there may be well-meaning concern for the well-being of the person in need without the necessary relevant technically competent performance. For example, parents may love their children but be incompetent for reasons of poverty, mental illness, or physical ill-health to take competent care of those children. It is in this sad situation that the state enters to provide alternative, hopefully more competent care of the children.[3] Indeed, with regard to both competence and fiduciary responsibility in a great many important areas, the state has set up a whole set of more or less effective alternatives: licensing, monitoring, and investigative agencies. Government has intervened where individual action is not sufficient to produce trust.

Some Limited Definitions and Defective Examples

The following cases make concrete the goals of this investigation of what we have called intellectual pursuits. As we examine just a few of the multitude of possible examples of the vagueness, diversity, and inadequacy in the usage of the term "intellectuals," we do so not to expose muddle-headedness or folly for their own sake, but to learn what we can from these examples about what we need to do to clarify

---

3. For my work on fashion and trust, see, on trust, Bernard Barber, *The Logic and Limits of Trust* (New Brunswick, NJ: Rutgers University Press, 1983); and on fashion, two articles, " 'Fashion' in Science," [1968], and " 'Fashion' in Women's Clothes and the American Social System," [with Lyle Lobel, 1952], both now reprinted in Bernard Barber, *Constructing the Social System* (New Brunswick, NJ: Transaction, 1993).

our subject.[4] Each of the authors of these texts on intellectual pursuits that are scrutinized closely exemplifies one or more of the shortcomings I intend my analysis to overcome. It shall be specified, therefore in each case what the shortcomings are and how we might overcome them. Examples are taken from a variety of current sources, the variety itself illustrating how widespread is the confusion we seek to clarify.

To start, before proceeding to the examples, can we learn anything from a good dictionary such as the *The Random House Dictionary of the English Language* (second edition, unabridged)? Of course, dictionaries have their own special functions, and they are not intended to be at the cutting edge of sociological analysis and innovation. But perhaps we can gain a few basic insights from the dictionary, for example, on the current diversity of meanings. It turns out that there are ten meanings given for "intellectual," the first being "appealing to or engaging the intellect." That, of course, sends us back to the definition of "intellect" pure and simple. There the first meaning is "the power or faculty of the mind by which one knows or understands, as distinguished from that by which one feels and that by which one wills; the understanding; the faculty of thinking and acquiring knowledge." It is clear that intellect and intellectuals have to do with knowledge of ideas and symbols, but of what kind or kinds? The dictionary synonyms for "intellect" are "reason, sense, common sense, brains." That does not help us much, and we can see that one of our tasks will be to explore the diverse, often vague, and sometimes contradictory meanings of "knowledge." In the next chapter, on the intellectuals and culture, we shall explore that quite confused topic and offer a systematic but provisional list of functional types of "knowledge," the different types of ideas and symbols that intellectuals, when the term is being used vaguely, actually deal with and often conflate. I shall argue that these different types of cultural ideas and symbols require different types of intellectuals. Moreover, in talking about these different types of intellectual pursuits we need to be quite specific about the kind of intellectual activity to which we are referring. Scientists and ideologists are pursuing different kinds of intellectual activity, so also are theologians and philosophers, or music critics and professors of linguistics.

---

4. Everything said here about the inadequacy of discussions about intellectual pursuits applies equally to charges and critiques of anti-intellectualism.

If we go back to the other nine dictionary meanings of "intellectual," we get an additional bit of help. One definition tells us that an intellectual has knowledge, or the capacity to get it, to "a high degree." Or, in a related definition, we are told that an intellectual is "a person of superior intellect." That is an everyday, commonsense conception, but we shall see in the chapter on high and low forms of knowledge or culture (defined as the symbols and ideas that make up knowledge or culture) that it is important not to limit knowledge and other cultural functions only to the high forms of knowledge and culture generally. Nor should we, as another definition suggests, limit the definition and discussion of intellectual pursuits to those who pursue knowledge and culture in its more complex fields, such as "aesthetic or philosophical matters." Knowledge or culture include, as we shall see in the next chapter, a great variety of functionally important kinds of symbols and ideas.

One final dictionary definition is important for our purposes of clarification, telling us that an intellectual fills a certain kind of socially structured role, "a person professionally engaged in mental labor, as a writer or teacher." But I shall assert, to the contrary, that while some people are intellectuals full time and holding to certain standards of professional expertise and responsibility, everyone in society, in all parts of it, has to deal with various kinds of ideas and symbols at least to some extent and at least some of the time, with varying amounts of expertise. In that measure, strange as it may seem to common sense, everyone has to have some capacity and functions as an intellectual. The dictionary, then, gets our ball rolling, but it leaves us with only some vague and diverse understanding of the nature of intellectual pursuits.

In the rest of this chapter, we turn away from the dictionary to explore a series of uses of the term "intellectual" that occur in some recent essays and books by and about intellectuals. There is no lack of interest, much of it passionate interest, in this subject in both the high and middle levels of the knowledge or symbol hierarchy that prevails in modern society. I cannot stress too strongly that the examples I have selected are only a few of the myriad of possible candidates for our clarificatory purpose.

An Avowed Intellectual on Intellectuals

We start with a statement in a book by an avowed intellectual that is actually all about intellectuals yet explicitly disavows any precise definition of what an intellectual is. The book is *No Respect: Intellectuals and Popular Culture*[5] by Andrew Ross, a professor of English at New York University. As we shall note along the way, those who explicitly call themselves intellectuals and write about intellectuals are often professors or specialists in the so-called humanities, an area that includes language, literature, and philosophy. Specialists in such other forms of knowledge as natural science, social science, art, and theology are not nearly so likely to call themselves intellectuals, even when they are proclaiming ideas functionally similar to those of their humanities colleagues.

Here is Ross's disavowal: "Just as the claim for any purity in cultural politics is suspect, so my own history of intellectuals is methodologically governed by no strict or absolute definition of the role or function of intellectuals." Indeed, Ross is proud of the inclusiveness of his company of subjects.

It includes, among others, Lenny Bruce, Ethel Rosenberg, Andy Warhol, John Waters, and Grace Jones, just as it includes Dwight MacDonald, Susan Sontag, Marshall McLuhan, Amiri Baraka, and Andrea Dworkin. . . . the diversity of the gathering is hardly surprising if one acknowledges the enormous difference in style between intellectuals of the Old Left, bohemian intellectuals of the Underground subcultures, the counterculture, and the New Left, Pop intellectuals and celebrities, and, lastly, intellectuals of liberation movements—the four, primarily generational movements with which I deal. To do justice to the respective spirit of each, it seemed necessary at times to refuse any high theoretical ground or vantage point from which an entire historical trajectory could be summed up, and to enter the fray.[6]

---

5. New York: Routledge, 1989.

6. Ibid., 10–11. For a more recent account of New York intellectuals that describes their diversity without giving any clear definition of their essential function, see the long article by Janny Scott, "90s Salons for New York Intellectuals," *New York Times*, April 20, 1996, 1, 24. Among the large numbers of circles, clubs, or salons, as Scott variously calls them, are: a group of older, conservative writers and editors"; "a loose circle of young magazine writers"; "a roomful of young fiction

Professor Ross does indeed have interesting things to say about the individual members of his gallery of characters, who come from so many fields of culture and from quite different high and low levels of culture, but it is my view that he could have profited from having some "high theoretical ground or vantage point" from which to discuss the quite different types of ideas and symbols, functions, and roles of his multitude of undifferentiated intellectuals. A theoretical ground would have permitted him to specify both the functional differences and the similarities among this motley group. It would have permitted him some solid ground for analysis or speculation of the relations of both congeniality and tension among them. Surely people as different in so many ways as the philosopher-critic Susan Sontag and the comedian-critic Lenny Bruce, as the feminist Andrea Dworkin and the black nationalist Amiri Baraka, need to be distinguished from one another if they are to be understood. He might have been able to "sum up" more confidently, perhaps, an "entire historical trajectory." With a clearer understanding of the variety and complexity of intellectual pursuits, he might have discovered both some underlying similarities and striking divergencies in that "historical trajectory."

On Black Intellectuals

Another confused and confusing omnibus discussion of intellectuals can be found in Michael Berube's article, "Public Academy,"[7] the main point of which can be read in its subtitle: "A new generation of black

---

writers, screenwriters, editors, and publishing industry types"; a "group of writers with interests in boxing, policing, and politics"; a "talk tank" of diverse types at the conservative Manhattan Institute; a "sub-group" of writers who do "critical essays" in magazines like *The New Republic* and *The New Yorker*; "another circle of writers and editors" who are "politically contrarian and skeptical about ideology"; and a long-lasting small group of people in a "reading circle" who started twenty-five years ago with Proust and have moved on to Tolstoy, Dostoyevsky, Balzac, Flaubert, Stendhal, Mann, Faulkner, Austen, Trollope, and then Proust again.

This article usefully notes the migration of many of these different intellectual types into academia and publishing, leaving fewer "freelance" intellectuals.

7. *The New Yorker*, Jan. 9, 1995, 73–80. For more on the black intellectual, see Robert S. Boynton, "The New Intellectuals," *The Atlantic Monthly* (March 1995): 53–70.

thinkers is becoming the most dynamic force in the American intellectual arena since the fifties." That a new generation of black "thinkers"
of various kinds and dispositions has emerged in the last ten years,
there can be no doubt, but Berube does not tell us just what he means
by an intellectual or a "thinker," though his article has much useful
information that might help one to define and differentiate types
among his diverse subjects. It should also be remarked that there are
many non-black intellectuals who would dispute Berube's assertion
that their black counterparts are the "most dynamic force in the American intellectual arena since the fifties." For example, a whole generation of white conservative social and political thinkers has appeared in
this period, and it would be possible to argue that their mostly ideological influence has been greater than that of the new black intellectuals.
What does "dynamic" mean anyway?

Berube begins by presenting some evidence that blacks have been
writing books that are getting national attention. In a midwestern mall
bookstore, he reports, prominence is given in the Current Events section to books by Cornel West (*Race Matters*),[8] bell hooks (*Outlaw Culture* and *Teaching to Transgress*), and Michael Eric Dyson (*Making
Malcolm: The Myth and Meaning of Malcolm X*). West's book contains
back jacket blurbs by such diverse "intellectuals" as Angela Davis, the
former radical activist and now a professor in the history of conscious-
ness program at the University of California, Santa Cruz; the Reverend
Jesse Jackson, surely an intellectual as well as a clergyman; Senator
Carol Mosely Braun; and Chuck D of the rap group Public Enemy.
This last admirer is an indication of the connection between the
"high" and the "middle" and "low" segments of the black intellectual/
cultural hierarchy.

The evidence of published books and popular book sales is taken to
support Berube's now more accurate generalization that "a new Afri-
can-American intelligentsia has become part of this country's cultural
landscape."[9] They have become, he says, public figures, or, using a

---

8. For more on West, see *The New Yorker* (Jan. 17, 1994). Profile by Jervis
Anderson, "The Public Intellectual: Cornel West is A Rare American Cultural
Entity: A Serious Philosopher With a Popular Following—And Some Vocal Crit-
ics in Academe."

9. Berube, "Public Academy," 73.

vague term that has lately become widely used, "public intellectuals."[10] It should be noted that in general discourse it is not clear whether public intellectuals are people who are known to the public or people who comment on a great variety of policy issues of great public import and attention. The term is commonly used in both senses. Whether "public intellectual" is a full-time or part-time role is also not specified, nor whether public intellectuals are always connected with universities or are sometimes "freelance." All these possibilities are manifested in Berube's list of black public intellectuals, but we do not know which of them have which characteristics.

The black intellectuals are said to have a constituency, not precisely specified, and they come primarily from the law schools and humanities departments of the formerly all-white universities and from among black popular culture performers. In contrast, until the 1960s the few nationally known black intellectuals were the novelists Richard Wright, Ralph Ellison, and James Baldwin. Also in contrast, up to the 1960s there was a group of professional black historians and sociologists (O. C. Cox, W. E. B. DuBois, James Weldon Johnson, Alain Locke, J. Saunders Redding, Carter G. Woodson), scholars segregated in the black colleges and little known either to the general American public or even to the then more segregated black public.

Given his vague and overbroad use of the term intellectual, Berube does not hesitate to include in the new black intellectual community " 'activists' like Marian Wright Edelman, cultural critics like Stanley Crouch, Lisa Jones, and Darryl Pinckney, and poets like Essex Hemphill."[11] But the heavyweight of this new intellectual group is in the universities, and Berube mentions other distinguished members from the academy: Shelby Steele, Patricia Williams; Stephen L. Carter; Lani Guinier; Henry Louis Gates, Jr.; and Randall Kennedy. All these academics, says Berube, "have decisively rebutted the claim that academe has been the death of the public intellectual."[12] Once again, there is no definition of what a public intellectual is and how much an intellectual role might relate to the role of being a scientist or scholar in a univer-

---

10. Although lately widely used, the origin of this term is not known.
11. Berube, "Public Academy," 75.
12. Ibid.

sity.[13] This is a point to which we will recur briefly in several later chapters and at greater length in the last chapter.

Berube finally comes to what essentially characterizes his very diverse company of black intellectuals. What Marxism was to the New York intellectuals of the thirties, forties, and fifties, black nationalism is to the group he is describing. Black nationalism has been "the inspiration, the springboard, the template, but also the antagonist and the goad"[14] to his diverse group. In practice, Marxism as theory and practice was certainly one broad focus of much earlier intellectual thought and action; black nationalism seems to be just as broad. Indeed, Berube says, "neo-nationalism in a broad profusion of popular-cultural forms has had to be taken into account by the black intellectuals because they respond sympathetically to this black popular culture. This fact makes the black intellectuals different from the earlier 1930s–1950s white liberal intellectuals, who were most unsympathetic to popular or what they called "mass culture." For them, culture in general was more important than Marxism and they saw mass culture as the product, to be sure, of a harmful capitalist society, but as fundamentally a threat to their own central value, high culture.

Just as there is always historical diversity in many parts of the social structure and culture of a society, there are always differences among the intellectuals of a given historical period. In addition to the more liberal black intellectuals whom Berube has primarily in view, he mentions a few prominent conservative black intellectuals—including Alan Keys and Glen Loury—chief among whom is the economist Thomas Sowell. And even among the more liberal majority, Berube indicates in passing, there are conflicts and tensions. Some of them criticize oth-

---

13. Theodore J. Lowi, professor of government at Cornell University, has written a not very satisfactory, bitter critique of public intellectuals and the recent prominence given to them in the general media. See his "Media Fascination With Self-Styled Public Intellectuals" (*The Chronicle of Higher Education*, Jan. 27, 1995, Sec. 2, B1, B3). Lowi is angry with public intellectuals for their attacks on the university and its system of specialized scholarship. He implies they are shallow thinkers, giving excessive weight to some single concept that happens to be approved in the current "intellectual climate." They are "idea entrepreneurs," whose ideas are usually not new and certainly not systematic.

In this piece Professor Lowi seems to be more the public intellectual himself than a scholarly student of the current state of "intellectual" activities.

14. Ibid.

ers for not being primarily concerned with public policy issues, especially those that relate to the serious problems of the "black underclass." Some criticize others for having "crossed over," for having "sold out" to the powers of the white mainstream. Some black feminists criticize black misogynists like the rapper Ice Cube.

Such differences are not peculiar to black intellectuals. Differences occur in all intellectual communities and need to be described and explained by means of more precise definitions of the various kinds of intellectuals, definitions that require a fuller and better list and analysis of the many different kinds of intellectual pursuit that make up a culture. Such precision also makes it possible to specify both the cultural and social problems inherent in each type of intellectual function and the sources of conflict and tension between different types. I shall discuss just one important example of this last problem, that is, the continuing conflict in the universities between scientists and scholars on the one hand and ideologists and reformers on the other, in considerable detail in the final chapter.

Tony Judt on French Intellectuals

The two previous examples of the vagueness and confusion in discussions of the varieties and functions of intellectual pursuits have been from American materials. These common difficulties, of course, are not limited to the United States. We turn now to a scholarly book on French intellectuals that provides further opportunity to illustrate these difficulties and to foreshadow the improvements I shall propose in later chapters.

The book is Professor Tony Judt's *Past Imperfect: French Intellectuals, 1944–1956*.[15] France in general and Paris in particular are perhaps the classic location for self-styled intellectuals and for discussions about them, not necessarily because they are any more numerous there than elsewhere, but because they are so intensely self-defining there, so

---

15. Berkeley, California: University of California Press, 1992. This book was also published in 1992 in Paris in French. The American translation was done by the author himself.

highly visible and concentrated in Paris, and so noticeable to non-French scholars and intellectuals.[16] The term "intellectual" in France is a term of admiration, of praise, of acceptance. There seems to be no ambivalence about intellectuals as there is in the United States.[17]

It will be most useful for our analysis and commentary on Judt's book if we start with a lengthy quotation from the very beginning of his excellent introduction and then move on to a few other key phrases and points in later parts of the introduction.

Here is the first paragraph.

For a period of about twelve years following the liberation of France in 1944, a generation of French intellectuals, writers, and artists was swept into the vortex of communism. By this I do not mean that they became Communists, most did not. Indeed, then as now, many prominent intellectuals in France had no formal political affiliation, and some of the most important among them were decidedly non-Marxist (Raymond Aron is only the best known example among many). But the issue of communism—its practice, its meaning, its claims upon the future—dominated political and philosophical conversation in postwar France. The terms of public discussion were shaped by the position one adopted on the behavior of foreign and domestic Communists, and most of the problems of contemporary France were analyzed in terms of a political or ethical position taken with half an eye towards that of the Communists and their ideology.[18]

---

16. For the seriousness with which the French intellectuals still take themselves, see Derek Schilling, "French Toast," *Lingua Franca*, Dec./Jan. 1997, 21–22. This is an account of the great stir in Paris that occurred on the occasion of the publication in that city of *Dictionnaire des intellectuels français*, a 1,258 page volume edited by historians Jacques Juilliard and Michel Winock (Paris: Editions du Seuil, 1996).

It is significant that the dictionary's definition of an intellectual is a person who has dealt with cultural symbols of one kind or another and who has been politically committed and active with regard to those ideas.

17. For a brilliant up-to-date account of Paris intellectuals, see Adam Gopnik, "Cinema Dispute: French Intellectuals Square Off Over Liberalism's Current Defining Issue—Or Rather, Over a Movie About It," *The New Yorker*, Feb. 5, 1996, 32–37. The persistence of the pattern of visible and powerful Paris intellectuals is one of the remarkable aspects of French social structure and culture.

18. Further on the centrality of communism in Paris after World War II and the difficulties all this caused for the novelist Albert Camus because he would not join his fellow intellectuals in their pro-communist, anti-American stance, see the recent biography by Olivier Todd, *Albert Camus: A Life* (New York: Knopf, 1997).

First of all, it is striking that there is no explicit definition of intellectual, and Judt's list, "intellectuals, writers, and artists," does not tell us whether this is a single category, a set of overlapping categories, nor whether there are functional differences among them. Indeed, at one point, Judt uses the very loose term, "the thinking classes"[19] to refer to his intellectuals. Just as Berube in his article on black intellectuals defined his subjects by an orientation to a social problem, black neonationalism, so Judt is orienting his set of subjects to the problem of contemporary communism.

It is a virtue of Judt's statement that he points out that intellectuals may be important without having "formal political affiliation." Intellectuals and their various locations and guiding ideas in different social systems, we shall see, are important problems in their own right. And it is a further virtue to point out, as Berube did with regard to the neonationalism of black intellectuals, that while a group of intellectuals may be "dominant," there are always, except in totalitarian countries, some intellectuals of different, even contrary, views from the dominant one. This dominance, Judt tells us, was in regard to "political and philosophical conversation," but he does not specify how broad a reach of social, economic, esthetic, or religious problems were involved. He does say, however, that the views of the intellectuals involved "ethical" positions and that these were "taken with half an eye towards that of the Communists and their ideology." There is, again, no definition of ideology but it seems to have something to do with ethical positions. In a later part of the Introduction, Judt says that his book is about the "apologias and their accompanying theorems" that were "espoused" by his subjects, an engagement that often "exacted a heavy moral toll." This emphasis on morality gets at another essential component of the concept of ideology. In the chapter on ideology we shall give a precise

---

19. Judt, *Past Imperfect*, 22. On page 149 there is still further evidence of Judt's confusion about intellectuals. He says, "Intellectuals are no better or worse than other people. They are not even very different." And there follows a set of statements that is partly correct and useful, partly half-true, but doesn't specify how intellectuals actually are different from other people, which is what we need to know. He says: "They live in communities, they seek the respect and fear the disapproval of others; they pursue careers, they desire to impress, and they revere power." Does this make them different from other people? I shall follow up on these points in later chapters.

definition of ideology that very much involves preference-and-criticism statements that are based on ethical, or moral, or value positions. "This situation," Judt goes on to say in his Introduction "was not wholly unprecedented." He compares it with the French ideological situation of the 1930s and begins to give what is a valuable part of his whole book, an account of the historical, as well as personal, factors that brought out the dominant procommunism of the postwar French intellectuals. Judt usefully compares the period of his particular interest with previous and later periods in France. And his account, of course, reaches beyond France itself, especially to what was happening in the communist world and in Eastern and Central Europe.[20] Unlike Judt, too much discussion of intellectuals is not sufficiently socio-historical and comparative. Such work is not easy, indeed often impossible, but it is in principle highly desirable to determine general aspects and patterns of the roles and activities of intellectuals.

A final virtue of Judt's book is that he is quite clear about the difference between scholarly history and partisan ideology. His book is outstanding as scholarship, as an objective account of his subjects in his chosen period, but he feels under no obligation not to make moral judgments about the consequences of their behavior and ideas. In a nice statement toward the end of the introduction he says, "one is not excused from the obligation to be accurate, but neither is one under a compelling obligation to pretend to neutrality." Or again, in a statement of an essential purpose of his book: "It is not a history of French intellectuals, it is rather an essay on intellectual irresponsibility, a study of the moral condition of the intelligentsia in postwar France." Judt here is finally acknowledging that he himself has an ideological purpose in writing his book. He is going beyond description to moral condemnation. The reader may disagree with Judt's moral judgment and may wonder whether this moral judgment has tainted Judt's historical account. But one has to admire Judt's clarity on the relation between objective scholarship and a moral, an ideological statement. In the last chapter we shall look into this general problem, the relation

---

20. On Russia and Communism, see especially Ch. 8, "The Sacrifices of the Russian People"; Ch. 9, "About the East We Can Do Nothing: Of Double Standards and Bad Faith."

between objectivity on the one hand and partisanship on the other, between science and scholarship on the one side and ideology on the other.

Representations of the Intellectual

As I have pointed out, the three previous texts exposing some of the ambiguities, inconsistencies, and limitations of some of the typical treatments of the subject of intellectuals and their various pursuits— Ross on intellectuals and popular culture, Berube on American black intellectuals, and Judt on French procommunist intellectuals—have not bothered to define what they mean by intellectuals. We turn, finally, to a learned and stimulating book that devotes itself explicitly and centrally to such a definition. The book is *Representations of the Intellectual*[21] by the distinguished literary scholar and very active intellectual-as-ideologist, Professor Edward W. Said of Columbia University. This short, exceptionally pithy book contains Said's 1993 Reith Lectures for the BBC. The Reith Lectures are, of course, one of the English-speaking world's most honorific series of annual lectures and have been graced by a whole set of illustrious scholars and public figures. Again, my purpose is positive, not negative; by pointing out the limitations, as well as the virtues, of Said's definition and discussion, we hope to provide a basis for a more accurate and useful analysis of the different kinds of intellectuals and the different kinds of intellectual pursuits in the later chapters of this book.

Like the scholar he is, Said starts by briefly reviewing some of the previous well-known discussions of the nature and functions of intellectuals by Antonio Gramsci, Julien Benda, and Michel Foucault, all standard names on this topic. But also as a scholar, and since a survey of the literature is not his purpose, he quickly acknowledges the enormous volume of writing by and about intellectuals that exists today and that he is not covering. This acknowledgment is worth quoting at length, since it should be a useful caution to anyone writing on intel-

---

21. New York: Pantheon Books, 1994.

lectuals; it certainly sums up facts and sentiments I have myself experienced and taken to heart. Said says:

Just put the words 'of' and 'and' next to the word 'intellectuals' and almost immediately an entire library of studies about intellectuals that is quite daunting in its range and minutely focused in its detail rises before our eyes. There are thousands of different histories and sociologies of intellectuals available, as well as endless accounts of intellectuals and nationalism, and power, and tradition, and revolution, and so on and on. Each region of the world has produced its intellectuals and each of those formations is debated and argued over with fiery passion. There has been no major revolution in modern history without intellectuals; conversely there has been no major counterrevolutionary movement without intellectuals. (10)

His task, Said is here insisting, is to get a better analytic understanding of the nature and functions of the intellectual, not to review the immense amount of often otherwise somewhat useful literature. That is my purpose, too.

Said highlights his own definition of what he considers the true intellectual by contrasting it with, and deploring, a set of roles and activities in the modern world often also defined as intellectual. "The world," he says, "is more crowded than it ever has been with professionals, experts, consultants, in a word with *intellectuals* whose main role is to provide authority with their labor while gaining great profit" (xiv). Surely this is an unrealistic statement. Does Said believe none of these activities is useful for others than the authorities in the social system, useful for any of a variety of the other values, interests, and groups that make up a social system? Does Said hold that there is no need for some authority in society? Does he believe that the authority does not need to be legitimated as well as criticized, both in general and in particular? We shall see that there are always intellectuals justifying the established social system in the large and in the small detail as well. Does Said believe that all these roles and activities are always rewarded with "great profit" and that, as he implies, "great profit" is the basic motivation for those engaged in them? In recent years, Said himself has been a powerful ideologist for the Palestinian cause. Surely this has not been because of "great profit." Said has been carried away by the rhetoric of argument and contrast.

Said's argument holds that the true intellectual is the dissenter, who speaks "truth to power" (note: power, which is illegitimate, not authority, which is legitimate), and who is often a marginal person or an outsider in society.[22] Intellectuals are "precisely those figures whose public performances can neither be predicted nor compelled into some slogan, orthodox party line, or fixed dogma . . . standards of truth about human misery and oppression (were) to be held to despite the individual's party affiliations, national background, and primeval loyalties" (xii). "Insiders promote special interests, but intellectuals should be the ones to question patriotic nationalism, corporate thinking, and a sense of class, racial, or gender privilege" (xiii). "There are no rules by which intellectuals can know what to say or do, nor for the true secular intellectual are there any gods to be worshipped and looked to for unwavering guidance" (xiv). Total independence is the hallmark of Said's intellectual. "Hence my characterization of the intellectual as exile and marginal,[23] as amateur,[24] and as the author of a language that tries to speak the truth to power" (xvi). Indicating his own moral and emotional involvement in his definition, Said says, "It is a spirit in opposition, rather than in accommodation, that grips me because the romance, the challenge of intellectual life is to be found in dissent against the status quo at a time when the struggle on behalf of underrepresented and disadvantaged groups seems so unfairly weighted against them" (xvii). And further, "It is a lonely condition, yes, but it is always a better one than a gregarious tolerance for the way things are" (xviii). And still further:

---

22. The sociologist Charles Lemert has written a strong and eloquent statement of approval of this definition of an intellectual by Said. He holds that this intellectual function should be an essential one for sociologists. See Lemert, "Representations of the Sociologist: Getting Over the Crisis," *Sociological Forum*, 11 (1996); 379–93. I shall discuss this view of Lemert's at length in chapter 5 of this book when I discuss the problem of tension and conflict in the academy, the strain between scientists and ideologists.

23. Said devotes the whole of chapter III, "Intellectual Exile: Expatriates and Marginals," to this matter. Said has, to some extent, himself lived the life of the expatriate and marginal.

24. See chapter IV, "Professionals and Amateurs," for a fuller discussion of professionals, amateurs, and the modern university. Recognizing the need for intellectuals to have some place in an established organization in the modern world, Said defines "amateurism" as "an activity that is fueled by care and affection rather than by profit and selfish, narrow specialization" (83).

The intellectual is someone whose place it is publicly to raise embarrass-
ing questions, to confront orthodoxy and dogma (rather than to produce
them), to be someone who cannot easily be co-opted by governments or
corporations, and whose *raison d'etre* is to represent all those people and
issues that are routinely forgotten or swept under the rug. The intellectual does so on the basis of universal principles[25] that all human beings
are entitled to expect decent standards of behavior concerning freedom
and justice from worldly powers or nations, and that deliberate or inad-
vertent violations of these standards need to be testified and fought
against courageously. (11)

I have not quoted all of Said's similar statements. Clearly, as the
redundancy of these already excessively numerous statements shows,
Said has a deep moral as well as cognitive involvement in his definition
of the intellectual. Said's intellectual is the pure ideologist.

Said's is, unquestionably, an eloquent, noble but utopian definition
of the intellectual. The role is located nowhere in society, only in a set
of values, in "truths," which are not specified but are presumed to be
self-evident. It reminds me of the similarly utopian vision Karl Mann-
heim had sixty years ago when he spoke of *"die Freischwebender Intelli-
genz,"* the "free-floating intelligentsia" he construed as a device for
transcending all partisan knowledge. Ironically, in his discussion of Julien Benda's definition of the intellectual, Said makes the valid criticism that seems to apply to himself. Benda's intellectuals, says Said,
have to be "powerful personalities" who

> have to be in a state of almost permanent opposition to the status quo
> . . . (they) are inevitably a small, highly visible group . . . whose stentorian
> voices and indelicate imprecations are hurled at humankind from on
> high. *Benda never suggests how it is that these men know the truth, or whether
> their blinding insights into eternal principles might, like those of Don Quixote,
> be little more than private fantasies.* (7, italics inserted.)

Said's basic mistake about what an intellectual has to be aside, his
discussion makes various useful points along the way. For example,
criticizing those who take a snobbish view of mass society, Said says

---

25. There is an apparent contradiction between this statement on "universals"
and a later statement by Said that in the modern world there is "an almost complete absence of universals" (92).

(xiii), "For me, the intellectual appeals to (rather than excoriates) as wide as possible a public, who is his or her natural constituency." Although he goes too far in seeming to condemn all "specialized" cultural discourse, he is justified in asserting that speaking as clearly as possible to the general public is an essential value in a democratic society. In the chapter on high and low culture, I shall argue that there are always people, often not called intellectuals when they address their ideas to the middling and lower levels of the public, who perform the same functions of providing information and justifying and criticizing norms and values as their counterparts do at the higher levels. And there is a lot of clear speaking at all levels.

It is another of Said's virtues that he will not stand for the denigration of all intellectuals. He speaks of "Paul Johnson's scurrilous, as well as hopelessly cynical, attack on all intellectuals" (xv).

And it is certainly a virtue that, despite all this moral passion on behalf of the miserable of the world, Said insists upon the intellectual's obligation to exercise "that critical and relatively independent spirit and analysis and judgment that, from my point of view, ought to be the intellectual's contribution" (86). And taking a more general stand against a prevalent moral and cognitive relativism among modern intellectuals, Said says, "But whereas we are right to bewail the disappearance of a consensus on what constitutes objectivity, we are not by the same token completely adrift in self-indulgent subjectivity" (98). However much he is the ideologist, Said is also perennially the scholar with standards of objectivity. Both intellectual pursuits are important to him, seemingly equally important. Unfortunately, Said does not discuss the inevitable tension and possible conflict that arise often between the independent and critical spirit of the scientist and the scholar on the one hand, and the impassioned intellectual-as-ideologist on the other. It would be good to know how he himself experiences and copes with this tension and conflict. I shall have more to say on this subject in the last chapter.

To sum up this chapter briefly, looking first at its negative side, it has shown the widespread confusion, vagueness, and inconsistency in the prevalent discussions of intellectuals and their pursuits. On its positive side, however, as I have suggested all the way along, it provides suggestions, for those with more systematic ideas, for numerous ways to clarify this complex topic. In addition to many minor points, several major ones have become clear. We need to have a better understanding of the different kinds of ideas and symbols that make up the realm of culture, which is the intellectuals' domain. We need to know a good deal more about what we mean by ideology, which is one of the chief kinds of ideas that writers who write about intellectuals, however vaguely, have in view. We need to know about what I have called "the hierarchy of knowledge," that is, the different high, middle, and low forms of each kind of cultural idea and symbol, from science to art and music. And we need to know about the tension and conflict that inevitably occur for those whom Lewis Coser called "men of ideas," when they try to combine different kinds of ideas one with another, for example, science/scholarship with ideology. This is not all we need to know about intellectual pursuits, probably, but I hope it will provide some improvement over our present knowledge.

Each of the four major points, along with many of the minor ones, is dealt with in one of the several chapters that make up the rest of this book. We proceed now to the first of these, intellectuals and culture.

2

❧ ❧ ❧

Culture and Intellectual Pursuits

In this chapter we begin our systematic study of intellectual pursuits by providing what the title of this book promises, a better understanding of culture based on social system theory. Such an understanding of culture is important for many reasons and absolutely essential for clear analysis and discussion of the whole variety of intellectual pursuits.

It is clear, both from the approximate dictionary definitions we have looked at and from the matters that discussions of intellectual pursuits primarily emphasize, that such pursuits are essentially about ideas, symbols,[1] meanings. In short, they are about culture, the set of ideas, symbols, and meanings that comprise one essential part of every social system. Unfortunately, this definition of culture as only one part of a

---

1. There has been a strong tendency in general discussions of the nature of culture to stress the verbal embodiments of cultural meaning and to neglect its visual embodiments in cultural symbols. A strong reaction against this tendency has recently appeared in a movement to study "visual culture." A valuable recent report on this movement says: "Typically, the rubric comprises researchers in art history, film and media studies, anthropology, cultural history, and literary studies, as well as philosophers and intellectual historians." The University of Rochester now offers a Ph.D. in visual culture. See Scott Heller, "Visual Images Replace Text As Focal Point For Many Scholars," *The Chronicle of Higher Education*, July 19, 1996, A8–9, 15, 16. An extensive bibliography on visual culture is included.

Of course, in principle, both verbal and other symbolic forms of cultural meaning are equal.

social system, which I shall develop more fully below, is not widely shared or clearly understood, contributing to a number of current confusions in the social sciences and the humanities in general, and not least of all in many particular discussions of intellectual pursuits. Instead of treating culture and its components as only one of the three partly independent, partly interdependent, essential structures of a social system, a good deal of current usage of the term stuffs into it not only ideas and symbols but also both social structural and personality components, these being the other two partly independent social system variables. This unsatisfactory usage can be seen in at least two important scholarly locations,[2] and by now also in much commonsense usage.

Confusion About Culture in Sociology and the Humanities: The Case of "Cultural Studies"

As to scholarly usage, first, and briefly, we see this unsatisfactory usage in sociology, where there has recently been what has been called "a turn to culture," meaning a turning away from the former strong tendency in sociology to social structural reductionism. Unhappily, this just means that one reductionism has tended to be replaced by another, that is, cultural reductionism. We find that everything, but everything, is called culture.

And second, we see this cultural reductionism with painful clarity especially in the humanities but to a considerable extent also in the social sciences, where what is now called "cultural studies" has been institutionalized as a separate program in many colleges and universi-

---

2. The recent widespread use of culture as a broad-gauge explanatory variable has come to the attention of the general press. In an excellent review, worthy of a professional journal, making knowledgeable reference to ten different professional and popular books and articles, *The Economist* has recently criticized the vague, reductionist use of culture to explain all present day worldwide social change and conflict. See *The Economist*, Nov. 9–15, 1996, 23–26. *The Economist's* critique is based on an excellent, if implicit, social system theory; it makes all the right, and specific, corrections of this current usage.

ties as a substitute for the disciplines of anthropology, sociology, history, psychology, ethnic studies, and much else.[3]

These cultural studies programs have been both enabled and created by aggressive publishing practices[4] and by the accompanying bookstore stocking and labelling practices. Calling themselves, not inappropriately, "cultural workers," editors at both trade and university presses now publish many mishmash "readers" in "cultural studies" for the numerous programs that they say are springing up everywhere. These miscellanies, these anthologies, mix together papers on such diverse topics as literary and social criticism, film studies, women's studies, ethnic studies, and more. And the bookstores do away with disciplinary sections such as those formerly labelled "sociology" or "anthropology" and now label them "cultural studies." The head buyer of the Harvard Book Store in Cambridge is reported as saying about the relabeling her store carried out a few years ago: "The store pulled all the mongrel titles from philosophy, psychology, sociology, and anthropology and placed them together in bookselling's equivalent of the time slot following *Home Improvement*. . . ."[5] But these practices worry another Cambridge actor in the world of publishing quoted by Boynton, Claire Silvers, publicity director at the Harvard University Press: "If you want to take the broad view," she says, "they could just put that name on absolutely every section of the book store." Cultural studies, as a result of these publishing and selling practices, has become very good business but not good for the theoretical clarity of the established disciplines of social science or the humanities.

Incidentally, it is not just in the United States that cultural studies now flourishes. It has become a worldwide intellectual fashion. In July of 1996 some four hundred scholars from all fields and from countries

---

3. For a comprehensive and powerful critique of cultural studies and especially of one of its now canonical papers, (Donna Haraway's "Teddy Bear Patriarchy: Taxidermy in the Garden of Eden," which has been reprinted several times), see Michael Schudson's "Paper Tigers: A Sociologist Follows Cultural Studies Into the Wilderness," *Lingua Franca* vol. 7, no. 6 (1997), 49–56. Schudson's critique is to be published also in a different version in a collection of essays edited by Elizabeth Long for Blackwell.

4. On these enabling and creative functions by publishers, see Robert S. Boynton, "The Routledge Revolution," *Lingua Franca* 5 (1995): 24–32.

5. Ibid., 27.

around the world met at a conference on cultural studies at the University of Tampere, Finland.

Given the lack of a standard and precise definition of culture, a definition of just what kind of phenomenon intellectuals are pursuing, I will do two things in this chapter. First, I will clarify the concept of culture, using social system theory. And second, since culture as a whole is made up of a large number of different functional components, we will briefly, all too briefly, discuss several of these, stressing the essential nature of each and its degree of independence both from other cultural components and from the social structural components in which it is always imperfectly and often transiently institutionalized.

The Concept of Culture in Social System Theory

Since the definition of culture used in this book is an essential part of the theory of the social system that I have constructed over many years, and therefore essential for a discussion of intellectual pursuits, it will be helpful to present the basic assumptions and components of that theory and show how the concept of culture fits into it.[6] This theory, like the definition of culture I will be using here, is different from much that is current not only in sociology but in the social sciences and the humanities more generally. It is my firm conviction that clarity and understanding about intellectual pursuits require clarity and understanding about the meaning of culture for social system theory.

"Action" as the Basic Stuff of Social Systems

The essential presupposition of social system theory is that its basic stuff is, to use what has become a technical term, "action"; that is, the exchange of meanings and ideas in social interaction through mutually understood symbols. Language, of which thousands of variations have been constructed in different societies round the world and over long

---

6. This whole section on culture and social system theory is heavily indebted to the discussion in my *Constructing the Social System* (New Brunswick, NJ: Transaction Books, 1993), especially the introduction to Part I and all of Part IV.

historical time, is the main type of symbols in social systems; but others such as pictures (as in art, for example), or musical notes, or mathematical notes, or bodily gestures (as in "winks and nods"), and various others are also often important as supplements or alternatives to language codes. "Action" is the basic stuff of the social world in the same way that "life" is the basic stuff of the biological world and that "matter" is the basic stuff of the physical world. All three of these basic stuffs are ontologically and theoretically coequal. Action cannot be reduced either to life, as biological reduction theories like sociobiology would have it, or to matter, as some old-fashioned geographical determinism would have it. All three stuffs are partly independent of one another, and each is partly and always interdependent with the other two. Of course, it is often extremely difficult, in any particular case or area, to find precise and definitive analytic statements and empirical evidence of how two or more of these stuffs interact with one another. Consider just the two cases, from many possible ones, of (1) mental dysfunction and (2) race, two areas where action theories and evidence often conflict with biological theories and evidence, with no satisfactory general resolution at the present time. Nonetheless, despite the difficulty of the theoretical and research task, because that task is fundamental for scientific understanding, scientists must keep undertaking it. And they do, endlessly. Scientific advance is often not easy.

Despite their difficulty, attempts to carry out studies of behavior that bring together knowledge from the three realms of action, life, and matter are often indispensable and valuable. Thus, when action theories and physiological theories were combined to study psychosomatic disease, knowledge and treatment were enhanced. My insistence on the partial independence of action does not imply any reductionism, only an assertion that action has its own analytic place in the understanding of social systems generally and intellectual pursuits in particular.

One last assumption: As we shall see in a discussion of the several components of culture, action has an essential value/normative component as one of its subsystems. It cannot be reduced to what is only one of its types, that is, to rational, utilitarian, individualistic action. On this assumption, both what are called exchange theory in sociology and rational choice theory in social science more generally and economics specifically are at best partial and at worst unsatisfactory for accounting for intellectual pursuits. Nor is action concerned only with the normative, as some critics of Talcott Parsons have continuously and erroneously alleged that he believes; the normative is only one element in action.

My multiple and complex assumptions about the relations among the three basic stuffs of existence, assumptions that are significant for natural science, social science, and the humanities, are graphically described in Figure 1.

Social Structure, Culture, and Personality in Social System Theory

To go on from the definition of action, the theory of the social system assumes that from the endless ongoing processes of action that make up any social system, the sociologist abstracts certain *structures*, that is, *relatively constant* uniformities or patterns in this process. We need to note that there is, unfortunately, little precision or consistency in most commonsense and even technical usage of these two terms, "structure" and "pattern." For the sake of consistency, I will use only "structure," not "pattern," which really means the same thing.[7]

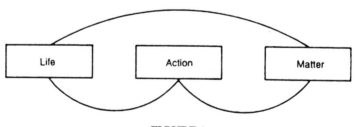

FIGURE 1
Relationships among Action, Life, and Matter

---

7. Because of the long-continuing influence of Ruth Benedict's classic 1930 book, *Patterns of Culture*, there is a tendency for anthropologists to prefer "pattern" to "structure," although there has been a contrary influence from the French anthropologist Levy-Straus's fundamental work on what he called "the structures of kinship." The result is no great clarity or consistency.

Structures—social structures, cultural structures, and personality structures—in the social system are endlessly being created through ongoing action. A good deal of the time, the existing standard structures are only being enacted, expressed, and felt anew, either practically automatically through learned behavior or through some negotiation of understanding between the interacting parties or through the use of sanctions to bring possible deviants into line. Of course, on the contrary, sometimes existing structures are being altered in small or larger ways. And sometimes, in what may be called small and large revolutions, wholly new structures are created. My assumption is that social system structures are basically dynamic; how and why they remain relatively stable, change slightly, or are altered in some revolutionary way is always a problem for sociological explanation.[8] Always, all the structures are the outcomes of interactions among a few or multiple actors.

There are three types of these structures that can be picked out from the welter of ongoing action, whether from everyday behavior or from our special present concern, intellectual pursuits: social structure, the basic unit of which is the role[9] (e.g., family roles, occupational roles); cultural structure, the basic unit of which is a symbol or an idea (e.g., a musical note or the word, "gene"); and personality structure, the basic unit of which is still unsettled among even action theory psychologists and even more unsettled between them and the biological psychologists. All concrete acts that make up the endless process of

---

8. In the last thirty-five years, the most original and influential analysis by far of the processes of cultural revolutions has been Thomas Kuhn's *The Structure of Scientific Revolutions* (Chicago: University of Chicago Press, 1962). Although, as the title indicates, Kuhn dealt only with the substance of scientific ideas, the change processes he described are applicable to all the other realms of culture where scientific and objective scholarship are carried on as important intellectual pursuits. In recognition of Kuhn's influence throughout the different fields of cultural studies, the philosopher Richard Rorty has recently called Kuhn one of the three most important philosophers of this century, the other two being Bertrand Russell and John Dewey. See Rorty, "Knowledge and Acquaintance," *The New Republic*, Dec. 2, 1996, 46–50.

9. Like other fundamental concepts of social system analysis, there is a considerable literature on the role concept, but a review of that literature is not relevant here. For a sophisticated discussion of roles and "role-sets" see Robert K. Merton, "Reference Groups and Social Structure," especially pp. 368–74, in Merton, *Social Theory and Social Structure* (Glencoe, Illinois: Free Press, 1957).

interaction have all three of these analytic structural aspects concretely intermixed.

Again, with regard to these three types of structure, I assume partial independence, partial interdependence. In principle all three are theoretically equal as explanatory variables. The existence of the three types of structure and of their theoretical equality is graphically illustrated, along with other matters to be discussed shortly, in Figure 2, which is a *provisional* theoretical model of the social system as a whole.

In this figure, because we read from left to right and may tend to think matters on the left are more important, we would be mistaken to think cultural structure more important because it happens to be on the left here, coming "before" social structure and personality structure. It is placed here partly to highlight it for our present interest in intellectual pursuits, in which cultural structures are a primary focus, and to counter the remaining tendency in much sociology to suggest that social structure is the most important of the three aspects of action. Position in the figure does not signify relative theoretical precedence.

The Functional Components of Social System Theory

Social system theory is a functional one; that is, it assumes that each of its three major structural types and each of the multiple substructures of each of those major types—as they are illustrated in Figure 2—have functional consequences for the social system. Both the major structures and their various substructural types have ascertainable consequences either internal to the system or with regard to the external physical, biological, and social environments. The internal functional consequences serve to maintain the relative stability of the system within itself, that is, as it is among its parts, or to create or respond to changes in some one or another part of the internal system so as to preserve relative stability or facilitate the changes that have occurred. The external functional consequences perform in the same way: they either maintain the relative stability of the system vis-à-vis its external environments or facilitate its adaptation to those environments when they change. My functional assumption, it should be noted, is intended

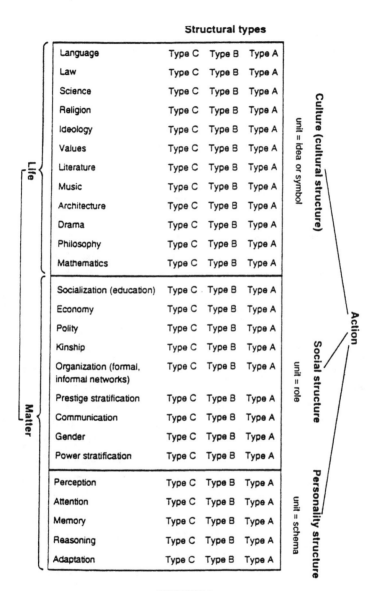

FIGURE 2
A Provisional Theoretical Model for the Social System

to account for both stability and change; it does not simply conduce to stability. As we shall see frequently in later chapters, stability and change are both characteristic of intellectual pursuits. The various components of culture contribute both to change and stability.

Some Functional Components of Culture

A basic reason for much of the confusion that occurs with regard to intellectual pursuits is the failure to keep essentially different functional types of idea, symbol, and meaning systems distinct. To give just a few examples, science is not distinguished from ideology, natural science is not distinguished from social science, philosophy and religious ideas are conflated, and values and rhetorical devices are assumed to be the same. What is badly needed in intellectual discourse is an analytic, comprehensive, functionally significant set of the types of meanings and symbols that make up that discourse. In short, what is needed is a systematic typology of the components of culture that occur in all social systems, understanding that the particular makeup of these components will vary in any given society over time and vary especially among different societies in time and place. For example, all societies have some of the rational empirical knowledge of the physical, biological, and action realms that we call science; all societies have religious ideas; but the amount and types of science, and the substance of religious ideas, may vary considerably, even as these varying types satisfy the same functional problems that call forth science and religion in all societies. Contrary to the view that "anything goes" in culture, however, our assumption is that its substantive variability is somewhat limited for reasons inherent in each of the cultural subcomponents. Just what these limits are and how they might be expanded is a matter for theoretical and empirical investigation.

It is important that the set of cultural components be defined in analytic terms, because often the different types may occur together in the same concrete intellectual discourse. Confusion is avoided if each participant knows not only which type of cultural component he or she and the other participants are using at any given moment, but when any of the participants is shifting from one type to another. Scientific statements and philosophical statements may occur together in the same concrete discourse; indeed, it may be essential that they both occur there to point out important relations between them, but it is also essential that the participants know when they are shifting back and forth between the one and the other. Otherwise, the individuals are confused and the joint discourse is confused. Even so sophisticated a scholar as Thomas Kuhn, in his enormously influential *The Structure of Scientific Revolutions*, was not clear about the difference between his sociology of science and his philosophy of science. As a result, for the rest of his career after the publication of *Structure*, he struggled with the problem of what he called "the incommensurability" of different scientific paradigms.

Specialists in particular fields of culture have devoted a great deal of thought and energy to defining analytically what is meant by their own type of cultural component, so that theologians, for example, may know pretty well what they mean by religious ideas, and literary scholars, similarly, may know about what they mean by literature in general or what is meant by one of its subtypes such as poetry or the novel. But specialists in one type of cultural component may well be ignorant of what is meant by other cultural components, and those with no special intellectual discipline may be greatly confused about the varieties of intellectual pursuits. Hence the need for an attempt to lay out a general and comprehensive account of the varieties of cultural components, an account that would be available to nonspecialists and the many different kinds of specialists alike. In addition to its theoretical significance for the theory of the social system, such an attempt should also be an essential part of what is called a general or liberal education.

The general account of the different components of culture laid out in figure 2 is intended only as a beginning of what such an account might look like. Although obviously based on a good deal of present knowledge about the components of culture, it is entirely provisional. Components may be added, or established components may be divided in a variety of useful ways. The set, or list, given in figure 2 should be the focus of widespread and continuing discussion and improvement. But it does make the essential point that such a general account of culture and its components would be invaluable for the improvement of cultural pursuits.

Some Cultural Components Specified

To suggest how such an account and an examination of the functions of some of the components of culture and the various problems and confusions that surround them might help, we now consider, all too briefly and superficially, but adequately I hope for present illustrative purposes, a few of these components. In the next chapter, to show what ideally would be desirable for each of them, we consider one of them intensively. That is the component of ideology, around which a great deal of confusion in intellectual pursuits occurs.

Science

We start with science, limiting consideration for the moment to physical and biological science, postponing discussion of their congener, social science, to the next section. I start with science not because it is any more important in principle, as my theory of the social system insists, than the other cultural components, but only because there is a great deal more consensus, both in the specialist and the lay communities, about its functions and boundaries. All societies, even the simplest, have some rational empirical knowledge of the physical and biological realms in which they exist and with which they have to cope. Human life is impossible without such knowledge.[10] Over the course of human history, this knowledge has become ever larger, ever more systematic. Although this trend toward increase and increased systematization, when viewed over long time spans, has been continuous, there have been some periods of particularly great growth. One such period began roughly in the seventeenth century in Western Europe and has continued in the modern world right up to the present time.[11] This is the period in which we have come to call such knowledge "science." What

---

10. For an extended statement of this point and of the development of such knowledge over the course of human history, see Bernard Barber, *Science and the Social Order* (Glencoe, IL: The Free Press, 1952), Ch. 1.

11. For a provocative discussion of whether the modern period of great growth of science has come to an end, see John Horgan, *The End of Science: Facing the Limits of Knowledge in the Twilight of the Scientific Age* (Reading, MA: Addison Wesley Press, 1996). Incidentally, one of the weaknesses of this book is a considerable conflation of science, philosophy, mathematics, and religion.

was once not named at all in a general way and then came to be called
"natural philosophy" is now "science" to all. In the nineteenth century, for the first time those who, full-time and intensively, and finally
as an occupation, pursued science systematically came to be known as
"scientists."

Science and its affiliate, technology, (I speak of "affiliate" because
technology is partly dependent, partly independent of science), while
dependent for their growth on all the other social structural and cultural components of the social system,[12] have had enormous reciprocal
effects everywhere in the social system. Indeed, incorrectly, science
and technology have sometimes been seen as the prime cause of all
modern social change. And further, in that part of the cultural component of philosophy that deals with the problem of how we know, that
is, in the philosophical specialty of epistemology, some thinkers have
asserted the doctrine of positivism. In an extreme version of positivism
it is held that there is only scientific knowledge; all else is ignorance,
error, and vague things called myths and superstitions. My own view
of the multiple independent components of culture contradicts such
positivism.

During the last one hundred years, so large has been the increase in
the substance, systematization, and resultant social structural and cultural consequentiality of science that there has been little basic intellectual challenge to its function and warranty as the type of knowledge
that understands the "real" empirical world. In the last generation or
so, however, such a challenge has come from a variety of sources, all
emphasizing the "constructivist" approach to science. From British sociology of science and from French philosophical and literary intellectuals, the constructivist assertion has come that there is no real world
out there for science to discover. "Reality," the radical constructivists
assert, is created by science and only by science; it is not "there," it has
no autonomy. Inevitably, this challenge has stirred great controversy
in the intellectual world. Its radically relativist ontological and epistemological claims are rejected when they are not ignored by working
scientists. As I have said, science is, of course, partly determined by a
variety of social structural and cultural components, but this is not the

---

12. Barber, *Science and the Social Order*, Ch. 2.

same as saying it is wholly created regardless of physical, biological, and social reality. Ironically, it seems to me that this relativist challenge to science comes out of the same basic source as science itself, that is, modern rationalism, namely, the attempt to explain all of culture as the result of rational knowledge. Like modern rationalism in general, especially in its philosophically overreaching and extreme forms, this challenge to science has affected and will continue to affect many parts of the world of intellectual pursuits.

Social Science

I have separated social science from its congeners, physical and biological science, not because it differs in principle but only because it is much less established in substance and much less legitimated among lay and intellectual communities than these congeners.[13] Indeed, there are those in both communities who consider social science impossible in principle, a pretentious claimant to the lofty prestige and taken-for-grantedness of the other, established sciences.

Yet it is clear that, like them, human life is impossible without at least rudimentary knowledge of how and why people in societies, small and large, behave as they do. Codified at its beginnings, and still so to a great extent, in folk knowledge (which is usually frustratingly vague and inconsistent, a mess of commonsense maxims), social science has made much slower progress than the physical and biological sciences. Of course, we forget that the physical sciences progressed more rapidly than the biological sciences and that biology has taken its equal place alongside physics only in the nineteenth and twentieth centuries, perhaps especially as a result of the recent discoveries of molecular biology.

Despite the great development of the history and sociology of science since World War II, the social structural and cultural reasons for the differential development of the sciences are poorly understood. Much more work, and also a better synthesis of what is known now, are what is needed to provide some tentative answers. One generaliza-

---

13. Ibid., Ch. 11, "The Nature and Prospects of the Social Sciences," for an earlier and fuller discussion.

tion is possible. All the different sciences have, over time, received some powerful resistance, as well as support, from a variety of social structural and cultural sources: think just of Galileo in physics, Darwin in biology, and Freud in social science. But it seems that resistance has been especially strong against biology and, even more so, the social sciences, because of their deep and immediate involvement with human values and interests. Right now, think of the resistance to the biologists' research use of fetal tissue or to physicians' "harvesting" (as opponents of this practice call it) of organs for transplant from terminally ill patients. Or again, right now, think of the resistance to social science research on sexual behavior, knowledge that would be useful in many ways, but is also repugnant and dangerous to many powerful people in Congress and elsewhere. Congressional opposition brought about the withdrawal of federal support for the University of Chicago-National Opinion Research Center national study of sexual behavior that was finally carried out, in reduced form, only with the support of private foundations.[14] A 1995 Congressional bill, the News Section of *Science* reports, "Threatens Child Survey Research."[15] And, most harmfully resistant of all to social science, a 1995 Congressional Bill proposed the total elimination of the social sciences from the National Science Foundation. Because of resistance from natural science leaders, the social sciences were not included in the original National Science Foundation. Gradually they were included, but now again they are threatened, this time not by other scientists but by members of Congress. Is it any wonder that the development of social science is slow and painful?

Whence the resistance to the social sciences? Because behavior is intrinsically normative in part, as I shall point out in the next section on values, social science research and the knowledge it produces can have large effects on people's values and norms and on the distribution of power and resources in a social system. Because there is strong commitment both to established values from some people and to proposed new ones from other people, those who hold these values develop

---

14. Edward O. Laumann, et al., *The Social Organization of Sexuality: Sexual Practices in the United States* (Chicago: University of Chicago Press, 1995).

15. May 12, 1995, 967.

strong justifications for what they approve, strong critiques of their opposites. These justifications are the ideologies discussed intensively in the next chapter. But the fact is that there is no end to the confusion and intermixture of social science findings and research on the one hand, and the ideologies that oppose and support them on the other. In the last chapter, we shall consider the special problems this confusion causes for members of the academy.

Scholarship

I have insisted that a prime condition for the clarification of intellectual pursuits is the construction of an analytical set of the different and multiple idea and meaning components that make up the culture of a social system. Science is such an analytical component. Before proceeding to discuss other such analytical components, I offer a brief discussion, by way of useful comparison and contrast, of what is commonly called "scholarship," a quite unanalytical and vague category that includes a wide variety of cultural pursuits.

Sometimes, but usually not even there, science is included in overbroad references to scholarship. It has definitely settled out as something different, its own creature, but with strong affinities with science. The term "scholarship" is intended to include everything else beyond science, every kind of relatively systematic research and study in the so-called humanities, from history through literary studies to legal studies. Although scholarship too often abjures being scientific, it shares with science the definitely modern will to be systematic, impersonal, and rational. However, it is usually highly ambivalent, when it is not flatly negative, about being cumulative, making progress, as science claims to do. We see this especially in the discipline of history, where historians at some point gave up the old German aspiration to describe the past "as it really was," and now declaim, even where it is clear that some cumulation has occurred, that history is endlessly revisionist, that each generation, perhaps each historian, writes his or her own version of past events. Historians will grant that facts accumulate, but not theories and generalizations.

This mild relativism of the historians has been transformed recently into the radical relativism that occurs in some history but much more in a great deal of literary studies, where the intellectual influence of French thinkers like Baudrillard and Foucault has resulted in so-called radical deconstructivism and thereby the relativizing of all literary texts. Where scholarship is intensive and systematic, but cumulativeness is rejected, nothing else is to be expected. Those who do not accept deconstructivism are now very much on the defensive, though strong counterattacks are also not lacking.

Because what is called scholarship, both on the whole and in some of its distinctive parts such as history, includes so many different kinds of idea systems, confusion and controversy are endemic. Sometimes the confusion is reduced when some part of scholarship, for example, linguistics, sets itself up as a science. But such movements are few, and confusion about just what kinds of idea systems are being studied prevails. Modern scholarship has produced many monuments, large and small, of certified and cumulative factual knowledge, but those who prefer to call themselves and be called "scholars" are mostly loath to claim to be scientific. The potential of this part of systematic and rational modern research is thereby diminished.

Values

Another analytically distinct cultural component of all social systems is values, which are structures of preference in the choices that confront all actors. All action systems endlessly, sometimes explicitly, sometimes not, confront actors with the dilemma of choice between or among alternative structures of preference. For example, should the actor choose to treat all those he or she interacts with equally or should he or she treat them unequally; as we now say in social science, should the predominant structure of preference be "universalistic" or "particularistic"? Or, to consider another common action dilemma, should the actor value rationality or irrationality?

The structure of values in a social system influences action at all levels, from interaction in small groups to that in the total society. This happens as very general values such as equality or rationality are made more specific in the form of *norms* for more specific interactive relationships. Thus, the very general value of equality in all situations is specified in the norm of equality between spouses or equality between parents and children. Systems of values consist of a hierarchy of general values and more and more specific norms. While values and norms pervade social systems, single values and norms are not exclusive determinants of action. They are limited and constrained in various ways. For one, different values and norms may be inconsistent with one another. For example, where the norm of equality between parents and children prevails, and where the norm of rationality also prevails, a parent cannot rationally treat a one-year-old child as an equal. In this case, rationality will prevail over equality. For another, values and norms have to compete with other cultural components and with social structural components of the social system. For example, the value of rationality competes with the religious doctrine of the primacy of faith: "credo quia absurdam." Or the value of rationality may be incompatible with the social structural requirement for solidarity in kinship, community, and national groups. While values and norms have their parts to play in the interaction that makes up social systems, so also do other cultural, social structural, and personality components. There is always a certain amount of incompatibility and resulting tension in even the most stable and harmonious of social systems.

Ideology

Since I intend an intensive analysis and illustration of the analytical cultural component of ideology in the next chapter, I can be especially brief here. Once again, I note that right now I am only pointing to the need for a systematic and comprehensive set of cultural components for use in the study of intellectual pursuits; I am not here providing full discussions of these several components.

Like values and norms, ideologies emerge from the fact of the need and possibilities for choice among alternatives at all levels of action systems. The choices actors make, their structures of value and norm preference, have to be justified; the structures of value and norm preference they reject have to be criticized as less worthy than the positive choices. These justifications and critiques are the ideologies that are as pervasive at all levels of society as the values and norms they are associated with. An ideology is not intrinsically a good or bad thing intellectually; it may perform its function of justification or critique well or badly, but it has its function to perform as much as any of the other components of the cultural system. Ideology should be a standard sociological variable.

Philosophy

Philosophy represents perhaps the classic case of a component of culture that started among the Greeks as an omnibus category including a considerable variety of idea systems and gradually, over the course of the centuries, has differentiated into a technical subject that deals with fundamental problems that belong to it and it alone. These are the problems of ontology, which asks what really is the stuff of which the world consists; of epistemology, or how we get to know anything about this ontological reality; and of moral philosophy, or the problem of whether ontology includes a basic moral aspect and what this moral aspect is.

Among the Greeks, who established the omnibus variety of philosophy at a remarkably high level of abstractness and systematization, it included not only ontology, epistemology, and moral philosophy, but also what we should now call natural science, social and political science, religion, esthetics, and much else. In the mediaeval world, philosophy was concretely very much intermixed with the theology of both rabbinic Judaism and Christianity. It is only in the seventeenth century that what we now know as science is called natural philosophy; natural philosophy becomes explicitly called science in the nineteenth century. In the seventeenth century and later, concurrently with the emergence of analytical science, technical philosophy itself is developing, with great figures like Descartes and Kant signalizing its growing analytic autonomy.

In popular discourse, and too much even in the writings of popular practitioners of intellectual pursuits, the old omnibus meaning of "philosophy" is often heard. Often, when someone wants to know what another person's values are about almost any subject, say, schooling, or the family, or punishment, or whatever, he or she will say, "What is your philosophy about . . .?" Or, to take one more example, when Dr. John Gibbons, the presidential science adviser and director of the Office of Scientific and Technology Policy in the White House recently wanted to comment about Congressional hearings on proposed funding cuts for the National Science Foundation and the National Institutes of Health, he urged scientists to make the factual case against such cuts and concluded, "Philosophies change on the basis of what facts you have."[16] Intellectual discourse would be improved by more accurate and precise use of the several analytic components of culture. An established empirical fact, a value or norm, an ideology, or some mix of these are to be preferred to the loose use of old-fashioned omnibus terms like philosophy. And that term, in its precise analytical sense, should be reserved for its own special realm.

Religion

In this brief and incomplete catalog of some of the analytical categories of culture, we end with the component of religion. As with many other components, the Greeks included religion in their philosophical discussions. When Christianity became predominant in the culture of mediaeval Europe, the balance shifted, starting with St. Augustine, and philosophy and much else were subordinated to religion or, as it came to be called under Christian assumptions about the nature of the transcendental being, theology, or God study. Since other religions than Christianity have different conceptions of their transcendental beings or principles, sometimes having many gods, sometimes having divine principles rather than gods, it is more accurate to use the more inclusive term, religion, rather than theology.

In Western Europe, in the modern world, the analytical study of religion differentiates out from science, philosophy, values, and ideologies. Religion becomes focused on the variable responses to what has been called "the problem of meaning." It is the problem that is inherent in the situation of human action, the problem that arises when actors have to confront the question not of what has happened to them but of why it happened, what the moral meaning of many inevitable events and situations is. Why is there evil in the world? Why death? Why illness? Why unexpected and undeserved bad and good fortune? Why human finitude? Why, indeed, human life? The study of religion

---

16. *Science*, 268 (1995), 1121.

reports both the existence of these problems of moral meaning and how various particular religions have answered them. All religions seem to include references in their answers to some transcendental being or principle that is the locus and solution of these problems. And all religions seem to have answers to what Christianity calls "salvation," that is, what humans have to do to become quit of these problems and enter into communion with the transcendental principle or being.

As an analytical component of culture, as a focus of intellectual pursuits, religion requires the most serious attention in its own right. It is a matter of ideas, symbols, and meanings, which may be associated with a variety of emotions but should not be reduced to emotions. Just because the ideologies and social movements of such varied historical phenomena as communism, Nazism, or capitalism have often been associated with very strong emotions is no justification for calling them "religions."

Conclusion

To sum up briefly, this chapter has defined culture as an independent and interdependent component of social systems, made up of ideas, symbols, and meanings of various kinds. The cultural system is composed of a set of independent and interdependent analytical idea, symbol, and meaning systems that badly need to be clarified and kept separate if the many different intellectual pursuits associated with them are to be improved. We have provided a partial set of such cultural components to illustrate the task and the problems that face an improved practice of intellectual pursuits.[17]

17. For an extension of and supplement to the analysis of culture given in this chapter, see Neil J. Smelser, "Culture As Social Process," in Neil J. Smelser and Jeffrey C. Alexander, *Social Diversity and Cultural Conflict In Contemporary America: Is Social Solidarity Possible?* Princeton University Press, forthcoming.

3

🌿 🌿 🌿

Intellectuals as Ideologists

lthough the cultural phenomenon to which it refers is as old
and continuing as social systems, the concept of ideology, indeed the very word itself, is modern. Born of the French Revolution and of Napoleon's disdain for his critics, the concept has become
pandemic in the language of modern social and political discourse.
Everyone is now in some measure and in varying rhetorics an ideologist or concerned with ideologies: the man in the street, sociologists
and political scientists, philosophers, and, of course, ideologists themselves, often called by various other names. There is, however, no clear
and agreed-upon definition of the concept nor of its functional role in
social systems. In this chapter I seek to remedy this defect in the theory
and practice of modern intellectual pursuits.

Ideology Defined as a Sociological Concept

Ideology is an essential functional component of the culture of every
social system.[1] Structures of ideology pervade every society. Their

---

1. For an earlier version of the analysis presented in this chapter, see Bernard
Barber, "Function, Variability, and Change in Ideological Systems," in Bernard
Barber and Alex Inkeles, eds., *Stability and Social Change*, (Boston, MA: Little,
Brown, 1971). This essay is reprinted in Bernard Barber, *Constructing the Social
System*, (New Brunswick, NJ: Transaction Books, 1993). Not only the central ideas
but sometimes the very language of this essay is borrowed for the present chapter.

function is to justify or criticize the values and norms of both the society as a whole and each and all of its parts, from large organized groups down to the merest dyad, the merest interacting pair such as spouses, friends, or colleagues who have their own special values and norms for their relationship. Ideologies are uttered constantly by everyone as a part of informal daily life, but often also the social structure of a society has occupational roles for ideological specialists. In this chapter we begin by examining intensively and analytically the functions of ideology in social systems and indicate why some individuals called intellectuals might more precisely be called ideologists. Extensive empirical illustration is provided of some ideologies that pertain to social systems as wholes, others that pertain to various parts and subsystems of society, and still others that exemplify their omnipresence among ordinary people in everyday life.

To begin, I recognize that this attempt to give a precise sociological definition of ideology in functional terms encounters a present situation of confusion and resistance. There is confusion because the term is so variously, vaguely, and often emotionally used. Indeed there is a whole set of widely used alternative terms for what are essentially ideologies; these alternative terminologies add to the confusion: "mythologies," "dreams," "fables," "apologies," "beliefs," "mystiques," "rhetorics," are just a few of those in common use. And there is resistance, especially in the United States, but also more generally in the noncommunist western world, because of the strong and close association of the term "ideology" with Marxist theory. Because ideology has been a good word for Marxists, it has been a bad word for non-Marxists. In the U.S.S.R., there were official governmental bureaus and occupational roles for the creation and diffusion of ideology. Such acceptance of official, government-mandated ideology is unthinkable in the United States. (Of course, unofficial, not-so-named ideologies stream forth from both the Executive and Legislative branches.) In addition to this Marxist taint from the Russian system, there tends to be a certain positivistic disdain among intellectuals outside Russia for ideology and ideologists: they are considered not scientific; they are considered the products of ignorance, error, and uncontrolled emotion. This, despite the omnipresence of ideologies called by other names.

How then can ideology be defined most usefully for sociological and more broadly social-science purposes? How can the concept of ideology be rescued from the ideologists for usefulness in social analysis? There is a need for a scientifically neutral place for ideology in the lexicon of social science.

We start with the fact, already mentioned in the last chapter, that one other essential component of every culture is some more or less coherent structure of ideas that are called values and norms. Values are the more general *patterns or structures of preference* that groups and individuals use in making the unavoidable and endless decisions that confront them all the time. Life and action are endless processes of facing dilemmas, of choosing between alternative courses of action. To choose equality or inequality, to prefer rationality to irrationality, to prefer a large family to a small family, these and other choices among limited but sometimes similar, sometimes opposite and conflicting possibilities, are what actors in social systems as wholes and in their several parts of the wholes face.

Norms are the specific applications of the more general values. For example, in an egalitarian and universalistic society, what norms expressive of these general values are to be applied by parents to a set of their children? Should the norm be inegalitarian primogeniture, as it has been in many past societies, with inheritance chiefly by the eldest, or should there be equal inheritance among all the siblings? Generally egalitarian societies, of course, lean toward the norm of equality for all offspring. The culture of a social system is in part an enormous interconnected web of values and norms that operate, along with other social structural and cultural components of the social system, to determine decisional outcomes.

Given that the culture is in part such an interconnected web of values and norms, it is clear why every individual member of the society, sharing, through long and intensive processes of informal socialization and formal education, as he or she does in its values and norms, is in some measure and occasionally an ideologist. Often actors make value and norm choices without being terribly self-conscious about this quite continuous and normal aspect of their actions, sometimes they more slowly and cautiously negotiate and justify ideologically which way they will go.

The Emergence of Occupational Specialists in Ideology

And it should also not surprise us that, as social systems become more complex and differentiated, some individuals become full-time ideological specialists. These specialists may be called by different names, even when they pursue the same functional activities. They may, as they often are in our society, be called intellectuals (latterly, "public intellectuals") when they are justifying or criticizing the more general values and higher-order norms and social policies embodying those values and norms. Or they may be called, in societies disdaining the terms ideology and ideologist, by a variety of other euphemistic, evasive, or wastebasket terms, for example: public relations personnel; newspaper, radio, and TV "columnists"; company spokespersons; "spin doctors";[2] social critics; social philosophers; staff aides; speech writers; or editorial writers; anything but plain and simple ideologists, which is functionally what they may be, in whole or part. The invidious term "ideologist" is avoided by these terms but there is no great clarification of what essential intellectual pursuit is actually being carried on.

How We Identify Ideologies

We recognize an ideology not by its content but by its function of justifying or criticizing a value, a norm, or an action decision that embodies the value or norm. We look for its consequences, for its normative effect either on the speaker himself or on his audience. Sometimes it is easy to ascertain the normative effects of an ideology: the speaker or the audience explicitly states that it is their value or norm preferences that are at issue. But sometimes it is not, when explicit statements of this kind do not occur. We can only correctly ascertain the existence

---

2. For a brilliant analysis of "spinning" as a contemporary political phenomenon, see Michael Kinsley, "True Lies: What's The Difference Between Spinning and Lying? Or Are James Carville and Mary Matalin Too Dizzy to Remember?" *The New Yorker*, Sept. 26, 1994, 48–53.

In the 1997 movie, "Wag the Dog," Robert DeNiro and Dustin Hoffman act out an extreme send-up of spinning at the Presidential level.

of an ideological function, intended or unintended, in such cases, by probing for a declaration of intent from the speaker.

We should also be aware of another difficulty, the one that occurs when speaker and audience have different intentions and responses. Thus, for example, professors are aware that in their teaching they may make what they intend as objective scientific statements, say about gender or race or ethnic differences, that are heard by their students as statements of value or norm preference, that is, as ideologies. Such differences of understanding are also not uncommon in everyday discourse. Analysis of dialogue, and writing too, and their functions is, of course, in general filled with difficulties. The analysis of ideologies is no exception.

Just because it is the functional effect that is important, the substantive content of ideologies can be extremely variable. Ideological statements may contain, in different measures, bits of science, sayings from common sense lore, anecdotes, epithets, appeals to authority—in short, anything that serves the justifying or criticizing function. That is why it is sometimes hard to distinguish between science and ideology. In statements about genetic determination of so-called racial characteristics, for example, the same statement may be scientific or ideological, depending on whether or not it contains an expression of value preference, pro or con. Science becomes ideology when value approval or disapproval is built upon it. We all know that the line between science and ideology may sometimes be hard to draw, more often of course for social science but also for physics and biology.[3] This is a matter we shall examine more fully in chapter 5.

Further as to the content of ideologies, we should also note that value-justifying and -criticizing statements are often intermixed in the same ideological expression. The intent in this situation is to strengthen the approval side of an argument by criticizing the disapproved value or norm. Thus, approval of equality, for example, is accompanied by arguments against inequality, or vice versa. Marxism does not merely criticize the inequality of capitalism ("the capitalist" vs. "the wage slave") but it describes and praises its own creation of a

---

3. For example, see R.C. Lewontin, *Biology and Ideology: The Doctrine of DNA* (New York: Harper Perennial Books, 1991).

breed of "new men" who will be both completely equal and completely free.[4] A dramatic statement of the positive-negative polarity of Marxism and capitalism can be found in Lenin's writing:

> The only choice is either the bourgeois or the socialist ideology. There is no middle ideology, and, moreover, in a society torn by class antagonisms there can never be a non-class or above-class ideology. Hence to belittle the socialist ideology in any way, *to turn away from it in the slightest degree*, means to strengthen the bourgeois ideology.[5]

Lewis Coser has coined the generic term "salvation abroad" to describe the ideological situation in which some intellectuals criticize their own society or historical period by praising some other society or historical period. The two examples he discusses at length are "the admiration for Russia and China among a wide group of French intellectuals of the Enlightenment and the Russophilia of English and American intellectuals during the 1930s."[6] As was seen in the report on Professor Judt's book in chapter 1, the French intellectuals of the 1930s and postwar period also had this Russophilia and its associated anti-Americanism.

In the opposite phenomenon that we may call "hell abroad," ideologists praise the values of their own time and place by criticizing those of another time and place. American Russophobia of the Cold War period produced a great deal of this hell-abroad ideology.

It is sometimes assumed that ideologies are always cast in an emotional tone. Not so. They may indeed sometimes be strongly emotional, for after all some value decisions are very important and feelings are strong in support of the value or norm chosen and in opposition to the value or norm rejected. In present-day America, in the conflict on the abortion issue, pro-life and pro-choice ideologies tend to be expressed with the strongest emotion. But an ideology may often be

---

4. For the Soviet version of the symbol and ideology of the "new man," see Raymond A. Bauer, *The New Man in Soviet Psychology* (Cambridge, MA: Harvard University Press, 1952).

5. V.I. Lenin, "What Is To Be Done?" *Selected Works*, Vol. 1, Part 1 (Moscow: Foreign Language Publishing House, 1950), 242. Italics in original. Note the taken-for-granted use of the term "ideology."

6. *Men of Ideas: A Sociologist's View*, (New York: Free Press, 1965), 143ff.

coolly and calmly stated; for some audiences, overheated rhetoric carries a negative weight. Ideologies are always addressed to both self and others, and their emotional tone results not only from the ideologist's own feelings but from his or her expectations about the response of the audience.

Some ideologies are being addressed not to an undifferentiated audience but by one ideological specialist to another. So-called journals of opinion are often the forum for this kind of dialogue among specialists. In this situation, professional pride operates to determine how the speaking or writing ideologist addresses his professional opponents. He or she will seek to gain the opponents' technical respect, even while expressing value differences. There is honor and pride among ideologists as well as among other professionals.

Like all the other meaning and symbolic systems of culture, ideology may come in more and less sophisticated forms (or to use the only available and rough scalar terminology of high, medium, and low) depending on its source and its audience. Since the general matter of the varying levels of sophistication of statements about all the cultural components, including ideology, will be the subject of the next chapter, little more will be said about it here. But high, middle, and low versions of the same ideology often coexist.

Ideology and the Rest of Culture

Although ideology is a persisting cultural function in all social systems, the relationships that its concrete expressions have with the concrete expressions of the other cultural components in a social system have evolved over time. Like so many other aspects of modern social systems, they have to some extent been differentiated out from these other cultural components, but not unaffected by them. Just as science, philosophy, theology, and art have been to a considerable extent differentiated from one another, so also has ideology. In primitive societies, or even in a society as undifferentiated as early, Homeric Greece, the "myths," e.g., *The Iliad* and *The Odyssey*, recited around family hearths, military campfires, and in public forums, are a concrete mixture of what the sociological analyst can see to be relatively undifferentiated concrete amalgams of poetry, history, science, cosmology, philosophy, religion, and ideology.

Along with differentiation processes occurring everywhere else in modern social systems, ideologies tend to become concretely differentiated out from other cultural systems, starting in the early nineteenth century and continuing all through the twentieth century. When intellectuals refer to the modern world as an "age of ideology," they may be referring to this increased concrete differentiation. It may or may not be the case that there is more ideology in the sociological sense than there was in the past, in other types of society. Probably there is, though measurement would be difficult if not impossible. Probably there is more because a more differentiated society produces more choice points for groups and individuals and there would be more ideologies for the relevant value and norm preferences. Differentiation is never absolute and is often difficult to achieve, as social science discovers as it tries to differentiate itself from ideology and other cultural components of the social system.

Ideological Change

Like all the other components of the social system, social structure and cultural structure alike, ideologies have not only a certain degree of autonomy but some tendency to change. Ideologists have a stake in making their ideologies more effective in preserving the status quo or changing it. For example, in the modern world, ideologists not only for the general value of equality but for specific equality norms in many different areas of the social system have been endlessly and effectively at work. Equality for racial and ethnic groups, equality for women, equality for children and the elderly, equality for medical patients and research subjects, all these and more have been urged by powerful ideologists who can effectively refer to the general value of equality and to evidence of present inequality in each of these areas to support specific norm changes. Active ideological agents can point to established social defects that have been taken for granted. As sociologists pointed out long ago, active ideologists can "make" new "social problems." They can try to establish new "rights." The result has been not only many different norm changes but also vast associated social structural and cultural changes. Internal changes in ideologies and the activities of intellectuals as ideologists are an aspect of social structural and cultural change that deserves careful study.

Moreover, since social change in general, wherever it occurs in the other social structural or cultural components of social systems, usually involves change of values and norms as well, we can expect a great deal of ideological discourse when social change in any area of the social system is at issue or is occurring. In the ongoing processes of social systems, there is a continuing mixture of ideological justification and criticism of the established social structural and cultural systems and practices and a counterpart continuing mixture of ideological justification and criticism of proposed changes in the established systems. Ideologies are always only one factor in social change, of course, but they have their part to play. For example, the ideologies for and against major modern types of social system such as those about capitalism and socialism/communism have been of enormous importance in the transformation of the modern world, always, of course, interacting with a variety of other social structural and cultural factors. The Marxist reduction of the source of social change to material factors alone is wrong in theory and has proved to be false in historical fact. I repeat, while we have to understand each and all of the many different cultural components that intellectuals devote themselves to, we have to understand the multivariate nature of social systems and not reduce analysis to a single component, ideology or any other.

No End to Ideology

As a conclusion to the analytic discussion of the functions of ideology, I might point out that the seemingly general view, propounded some thirty years ago, that the world was seeing an "end of ideology" is clearly wrong. There can be no end of ideology in social systems. Those who proposed the "end of ideology" were provincially talking only about a particular case, Marxist and Russian ideology, and even in that limited case it was highly questionable. Fortunately, that view is no longer heard, but unfortunately, it is still a fact that the general sociological functions of ideology are too little understood. Since ideologies are here to stay, we need to understand them better.

Some Empirical Illustrations of the Activities of Ideologists and the Functions of Ideologies

As promised earlier in the chapter, we turn now to a set of empirical illustrations of some of the analytical points about ideologists and ideologies made up to this juncture. We start with a biography of a celebrated intellectual as ideologist, a biography that has many typical features of the careers and activities of other present-day intellectuals as ideologists.

A Biography of an Intellectual as Ideologist

One of the most celebrated intellectuals as ideologist of the late twentieth century in the United States is William J. Bennett, whose celebrity has extended to having a profile by Michael Kelly about him in *The New Yorker* magazine, which is read by many intellectuals of many different kinds.[7] This profile, to which the following account has a large debt, has a somewhat hostile or at least skeptical tone, since its subhead is "The Man of the Minute," implying that Bennett's ideological influence may be only temporary. The profile is not, however, actually skeptical about Bennett's long-term ideological activities or their widespread influence. "Morality is in," continues the subhead, and the script under a cartoon of Bennett describes him as "A leading voice of a force that is driving American politics—for now."

Bennett was the son of a middle-class Irish-Catholic divorced mother in Brooklyn, New York. "He grew up" says Kelly, "in a world defined by Democratic social moralism," very much a child of Franklin Delano Roosevelt's era of liberal ideology and politics. His conviction that society was fundamentally a moral order was built and strengthened by his attendance at Gonzaga High School in Washington, D.C., a Jesuit school with a strict moral emphasis and strong discipline. Al-

---

7. Michael Kelly, "The Man of the Minute," *The New Yorker* (July 17, 1995), 26.

though it might have been expected that a student like Bennett would then go on to a Catholic college, or even enter the intellectually oriented Jesuit order, he did not. Instead, for reasons that Kelly does not describe, Bennett went to the liberal secular Williams College in Massachusetts. There he engaged in such liberal activities as those connected with civil rights and fell under the influence, and took as his mentor, the very liberal ideologist and activist, the Rev. William Sloane Coffin. Because of Bennett's interest in philosophy and morality, Coffin recommended that he go for graduate work in philosophy to the University of Texas, then a center of liberal ideology and activism. At Texas he came under the influence of John Silber, at that time very much a liberal, even serving as faculty advisor to the radical Students for a Democratic Society; later he became the very conservative president of Boston University.

Although he took a doctorate in political philosophy at Texas, Bennett did not pursue an academic career but applied his talent for ideology and moral philosophy in nongovernmental, nonprofit organizations. During this time, his views took a turn toward conservatism, as he became disillusioned with liberalism. In 1981, probably in part as a result of this change in his views, when he had become the little-known president of a humanities think-tank in Research Triangle Park, N.C. (which is adjacent to the University of North Carolina and Duke University), he was appointed by President Reagan to head the National Endowment for the Humanities, even then coming under attack by cultural conservatives for its liberal ideologies and practices. It was in this position, only three months after taking it, that he courted great public attention by denouncing a federally funded television documentary on the Nicaraguan revolution as "unabashed socialist-realism propaganda" (read, "ideology").[8]

In 1985 President Reagan made him Secretary of Education and once again he immediately adopted a confrontational ideological stance by telling the president of the National Education Association, during a courtesy call from that spokesman (read "ideologist") for liberal education, that he intended to speak out against the Association because he regarded it as "a big part of the problem of American education."

---

8. Kelly, "The Man of the Minute," 28.

Bennett has never stayed very long with one particular moral cause or its ideological urging. In 1988 he was appointed by President George Bush to be the Director of the Office of Drug Control Policy, a position that was popularly known as the "drug czar." His large task was to state values and norms, formulate policies, and organize practices that would control the moral evil of drug use in the United States. After two years Bennett resigned from that unfinished task and has since been a co-director of an organization called Empower America (whose co-director is politician Jack Kemp), a Fellow at the conservative Heritage Foundation, and an editor of *National Review* magazine, one of the earliest of the conservative ideology journals of opinion, founded by William Buckley, who has been a powerful conservative ideological voice on the *Review* and elsewhere for forty years.

These are apparently secondary attachments; mostly Bennett has devoted himself to freelance writing and well-paid lecturing to conservative groups. He remains a prominent national figure able to get national attention for whatever particular moral cause he chooses to speak out on.

But Bennett is not interested just in single, particular moral issues. He has become the passionate ideologist for a general conservative set of values and norms, a set that he himself has been ideologizing for during the last two decades. He sees himself as the spokesman for a moral society, a society with, among other characteristics, a strong family, without a drug epidemic, with an effective system of moral and general education, a "wholesome" popular culture, and in general, "a good character." His values and ideologies overlap with but are not identical to those of the conservative Moral Majority.

Within the community of intellectuals who are ideologists of one persuasion or another, Bennett gets a mixed press, criticism mixed with praise, but both usually based on technical respect. Kelly, the author of the *New Yorker* profile, is ambivalent, expressing implicit criticism by calling him a "pitchman," "a sermonizer." (Note the almost endless variety of terms for "ideologist.") But he shows his respect for Bennett's ideological talent by calling him a genius at addressing the middle-brow world. In the same positive vein, Bennett's extremely successful book, *The Book of Virtues: A Treasury of Great Moral Stories*, an 800-page volume that has been on the best-seller list for about a year, has been treated with respect by the more liberal journals of opinion such as the *Washington Post* and the *New Republic*. Its purpose is to provide materials by which parents and children can learn to be more moral members of the moral society that Bennett advocates.

Finally, the case of Bennett shows how, in contemporary America, the role of ideologist has not only become more clearly, if still not entirely, differentiated out concretely from other intellectual pursuits, but also that it can earn national prestige and sometimes considerable financial rewards. Bennett is said to have earned about five million dollars from *The Book of Virtues* alone and gets as much as forty thousand dollars for one of his ideological addresses to some powerful American business and professional associations. This order of financial success is probably unusual, but we can see that intellectuals as ideologists can now be both famous and well-to-do.

An Example of an Ideology for a Whole Society: Newt Gingrich's *To Renew America*

All societies have some more or less coherent set of central values and the more specific norms that express them in myriad particular behavioral situations. Except in despotic dictatorships, where the force of government controls is omnipotent, there is never complete consensus about these values and norms. (Even in the most despotic days of the Soviet regime in Russia, some dissenters expressed their different values and norms through the underground publishing channels of what was known as *samizdat*.) In democracies, one of whose most central values is freedom, and especially freedom of speech, there is more dissensus about even central values and still more about particular norms. Consensus on values and norms is one, and only one, of the integrating mechanisms in society as a whole and in its large number of subsystems. Value-conflict, as the United States saw most clearly perhaps during its Civil War experience, has disintegrative effects that can tear whole societies and their several parts asunder.

Since there is in principle always a choice among different values and norms, we have stressed in this chapter that ideologies function to justify or criticize the choices made. Ideologies for a whole society seek to show the part the values play in giving an identity and unity to that society. The justifying ideologies don't rest content with affirmative statements; they also often contain negative ones, statements that criticize dissenting values and norms and those who propound and preach them. The negative statements are intended to strengthen the positive ones.

The established ideologies are usually so frequently and commonly expressed that most members of the society take them for granted, accept them as unquestionable truths. However, in what are defined by some as times of crisis, there may be an efflorescence and growth of self-consciousness about the established ideologies. Ideologies issue from many voices: politicians, statesmen, the news media (print, radio, and TV), social commentators and critics, even clergymen in pulpits, and people in their everyday conversations, to name but some of these voices.[9] Sometimes it seems as if ideologies are omnipresent.

Certainly this is the case for the United States. A number of factors contribute to this condition. First of all, there is the value of freedom and free speech, enshrined in the Constitution and the Bill of Rights, and very much a strong tenet at all levels of society. Everyone feels free to express his or her values, norms, and supporting ideologies. Second, there is the widespread ideological belief in the United States that this country is what S.M. Lipset has called "the first new nation," in his book with that title.[10] As such, the United States has felt a special obligation to explain and justify its special values and norms. And, third, connected with this sense of a special identity, has been the continuing historical, political, and sociological discussion of "American exceptionalism,"[11] that is, the question of how and why America has indeed been an exceptional, even unique, society. This discussion has given rise to much social science analysis and to even more ideological discourse.

---

9. With regard to these many voices, Gingrich says: "The intellectual nonsense propagated since 1965—in the media, on university campuses, even among our religious and political leaders—now threatens our ability to teach the next generation to be Americans." In Newt Gingrich, *To Renew America* (New York: HarperCollins, 1995): 4.

10. New York: Basic Books, 1963. Anchor Edition, 1967.

11. See Seymour Martin Lipset, *American Exceptionalism: A Double-Edged Sword* (New York: W.W. Norton, 1994), for an outstanding analysis and history of this concept, which is partly quasi-scientific, partly ideological.

In this broad American social and historical context, the best-selling book, *To Renew America*,[12] by the politician, Newt Gingrich, now Speaker of the House of Representatives and a great power in the Congress as a whole, is not so remarkable as it has seemed to some. Moreover, Gingrich is not your usual politician declaiming what some staff aide has written for him (although he acknowledges assistance from a co-writer). Gingrich has, and makes claims to, a certain general intellectual background apart from his political role. He has a Ph.D. in history and has for some years taught a course, "Renewing American Civilization" at a small college in Georgia. At one point in the first chapter of his book, Gingrich says, "I have spent much of my life studying and working on the problems of how civilizations survive." Further, Gingrich is at pains in the first part of his book to refer to and cite more than a score of books and articles that have influenced his views on American society and its values and, indeed, on history in general. In this latter respect, he stresses the strong influence on him of two writers: the "challenge and response" theory of the historian-social philosopher Arnold Toynbee, a theory spelled out in Toynbee's ten-volume *A Study of History*, and the societal analysis and futuristic predictions of the physicist-science fiction novelist Isaac Asimov in his *Foundation* trilogy. As a result of his Toynbeean mode of thought, Gingrich's first chapter is titled "The Six Challenges Facing America." (Gingrich has a rhetorical fondness for numbered lists of topics. There are several of them in the book.)

Gingrich's title, *To Renew America*, states his central purpose, first to deplore the decline of American civilization[13] and its values, next to restate these values and their associated ideologies, and finally to derive from these values a political program for the first and following sessions of Congress in which the Republican Party holds the majority and he is its Speaker.

---

12. Gingrich, 1995. For a sharp critique of the substance and the rhetoric in this book and of the personality of its author, see Joan Didion, "The Teachings of Speaker Gingrich," *The New York Review of Books*, Aug. 10, 1995. The allusion in the title of the article to The Little Red Book of Chairman Mao is indicative of the author's ideological hostility to Gingrich's ideology and program.

13. Gingrich prefers "civilization" to "society," probably as a result of the Toynbeean influence on his thought.

The political program, called The Contract With America, is contained in a statement of ten (again, the list) extremely diverse legislative goals. Note that the term "contract" itself has strong positive value and ideological significance for Americans living in a lawful and market society, in which contracts are at the heart of much social interaction.

To show that a reaffirmation of American values and ideologies is necessary, Gingrich repeatedly claims that America is in crisis and in decline. For example, the first paragraph of the first chapter states, "our civilization is decaying." And in the concluding chapter, he says, "I did not write *To Renew America* to convince you that this anxiety is inappropriate. Just the opposite. I wrote this book to convince you that your future, your children's future, and your country's future is at a crossroads." Similar remarks are repeated throughout the book. Gingrich is the typical ideologist calling "crisis."

Before we look at Gingrich's positive statement on values and ideologies, we may note that, like many ideologists, he has important negative criticisms to make of views different from his own and of those who make them. Strewn throughout the first part of his book are criticisms of "elites," "academics," and "intellectuals." On the very first page of the book he says, "While we as a people were winning our battles round the world, here at home our elites were deserting us. For the past thirty years we have been influenced to abandon our culture and seem to have lost faith in the core values, traditions, and institutions of our civilization." A few pages farther on, the unspecified elites are charged with deliberate intent. "Since 1965," says Gingrich, "there has been a calculated effort by cultural elites to discredit this civilization and replace it with a culture of irresponsibility that is incompatible with American freedoms as we have known them." The elites are now specified to be "cultural," not business or political elites.

The cultural elites are further specified at the beginning of the section of the book entitled "Reasserting and Renewing American Civilization," as the "counterculture" and the holders of "multicultural," "situational ethics," and "deconstructionist" views. Gingrich says,

> In the mid-1960s, the long-held consensus began to founder. The counterculture began to repudiate middle-class values—even though the creators of that counterculture were clearly middle class themselves.

Multiculturalism switched the emphasis from proclaiming allegiance to the common culture to proclaiming the virtues (real or imagined) of a particular ethnicity, sect, or tribe. "Situational ethics" and "deconstructionism"—the belief that there are no general rules of behavior—began to supplant the centuries-old struggle to establish universal standards of right and wrong.

'And Gingrich reports that when he began to read up for his course on American civilization, "The biggest surprise was to find how far most twentieth-century intellectuals have strayed from the assumptions and values of the Founding Fathers." Finally, these intellectuals are summarily described as "liberals." "By blaming everything on society," says Gingrich, "contemporary liberals are really trying to escape the personal responsibility that comes with being an American." Gingrich's theory of societal "decay" is clearly a cultural one; for his alleged decay and crisis he blames wrong values and ideologies, not political or economic parts of the social structure of the United States.

For all his penchant for making numbered lists of topics, problems, remedies, whatever, Gingrich has no list of central American values. The values he points to are strung out discursively, in various parts of the book but especially in the first part. There is no attempt at their systematic classification or explicit order of importance. Those he does discuss are offered as essential for "renewing" America; the chief ideological theme and refrain is that following these values will restore America to its former greatness, to preeminence in the world, and will preserve the well-being of his readers, their children, and their posterity.

Carefully scrutinizing his discursive prose, both for positive statements and the implicit statements in his negative views of "elites," we find the following core values and their associated ideologies mentioned.

First in the book, Gingrich stresses the value of freedom. "Will historians," he says, "record America . . . as the center of freedom that, having defeated its foreign enemies, found the moral and political courage to revitalize its civilization and lead the human race to even greater levels of freedom, prosperity, and security? . . . Once again, America would be the last best hope on earth." Invocations of freedom occur throughout the book.

Although he does not use the term "individualism" to describe one of America's central values, it has a key importance for Gingrich. As we have already seen in his criticism of liberals and intellectuals, they are accused of denigrating the importance of individual responsibility and instead stress "society," instead stress the effects of this supra-individual entity rather than those of its component individuals. In his frequent condemnations of individual irresponsibility and praise for personal responsibility and initiative, Gingrich is affirming the value of individualism. As he says colloquially in the first chapter, "However, as my grandmother taught me, God helps those who help themselves." Or more rhetorically and absolutely, "Democracies rely *only* (emphasis inserted) on the unique spark of each person's God-given talent." As we can readily see from his invocation of God, this value, and presumably the others that Gingrich considers essential to our civilization, are not merely secular creations but have a religious origin and support. He says,

> Our civilization is based on a spiritual and moral dimension. It emphasizes personal responsibility as much as individual rights. Since 1965, however, there has been a calculated effort by cultural elites to discredit this civilization and replace it with a culture of irresponsibility that is incompatible with American freedoms as we have known them. . . . Until we reestablish legitimate moral cultural standards, our civilization is at risk.

Probably not at the same moral level as freedom and individualism for Gingrich but still a very important value is "the tradition" of social mobility.

> We must replace the welfare state with an opportunity society. Every American is entitled to a life filled with opportunity. After all, we are endowed by our Creator with certain inalienable rights, among which are life, liberty, and the pursuit of happiness. Yet today too many Americans are bound in bureaucratic and antihuman regulations by which families are destroyed, the work ethic is undermined, male irresponsibility is made irrelevant, and young mothers find themselves trapped in a world where "income maintenance" replaces opportunity.

Clearly, Gingrich feels that individualism, responsibility, and opportunity are interdependent. That is the nature of core values, they interact and usually support but also may conflict with one another.

These then are the values and ideologies that Gingrich sees as central to our society. These are the values that he feels infuse the several legislative goals of his Contract with America, where they are embodied as specific norms. They are values and ideologies that are very much a part of American culture and, therefore, speak powerfully to Americans.

But there are other values that are perhaps equally important to Americans: the values of equality, of rationality, of justice and security for all in a lawful society. These are values that Gingrich does not mention. Both sets of values and their associated ideologies play their parts in the present political situation and will continue to do so in the future. Both by the values and ideologies he includes and those he omits, Gingrich seeks to define and justify the specific political decisions he wants his Republican Party to achieve.[14]

Environmentalism: An Expanding Ideology

Although it sometimes seems so, because of its present great popularity and scope, American environmentalism is not a recent development. In its various forms it has a long history, a history in which change and enlargement occur more often in spurts than incrementally.[15]

The values and ideologies of environmentalism began with a limited focus, the preservation of "the wilderness," and have developed so that they now cover a complex set of interrelated problems, not only in the United States but in the world as a whole. For example, the title of Vice President Al Gore's 1992 book, which has been a national bestseller in hardcover and in paperback editions, expresses its explicit ideological message for the whole world: *Earth In the Balance: Ecology*

---

14. For quite a different and contrasting account of America's values and ideologies, given in the context of her excellent history of the original making and eventual transformation of the Declaration of Independence, see Pauline Maier, *American Scripture: Making the Declaration of Independence* (New York: Knopf, 1997). From its very title and throughout the book, Maier's history illustrates many general points that we have made about ideology.

15. For an excellent brief but well-documented account of this history, see Daniel J. Kevles, "Greens in America," *The New York Review of Books*, Oct. 6, 1994, 35–40.

and the Human Spirit.[16] And the strong value and ideological message of the book has been noted and hailed in the national press with review phrases like "a strong thread of values and ethics," it "uphold(s) ideals," it is "passionately written," "a plea for moral responsibility," and "brilliantly written, prophetic, even holy."[17]

The first spurt of development of the environmental ideology occurred in the late nineteenth and early twentieth century. This environmentalism praised the value of preserving the remaining American wilderness as a refuge from the evils of growing urban dirt, disorder and greedy capitalists. Among its promoters were John Wesley Powell, the distinguished geologist and explorer; Theodore Roosevelt; the San Franciscan founders of the Sierra Club; Gifford Pinchot; and John Muir. Perhaps its chief accomplishment was the establishment of the national park system and of such state park systems as New York's huge, and partially "ever wild," Adirondack Park. The advocates of this form of environmentalism were predominantly white, Anglo-Saxon, Protestant, well-to-do male residents of Northeastern cities. Not surprisingly, then, this form of environmentalism has sometimes been characterized as "elite environmentalism."

The advocates of "wilderness preservation" environmentalism were joined by a group of what may be called urban environmentalists, who campaigned against the pollution, poisoning, and poverty of the expanding American urban workplaces and slums. Many of them were upper-middle class women who were working in the settlement houses of the slums to improve life for the slum residents. At Hull House in Chicago, for example, Jane Addams and her colleagues tried to improve ways of dealing with such local environmental hazards as garbage, sewage, water, industrial effluents, and horse manure, which was a principal source of pollution in its time.

As a physician working at Hull House, Dr. Alice Hamilton became so disturbed by the conditions she had to deal with that she became what may have been the first medical urban/environmentalist. It was an environmentalism for working-class immigrants. She investigated public health issues such as outbreaks of typhoid stemming from pol-

---

16. New York: Penguin Press, 1992, 1993.
17. These are reproduced on the first pages of the paperback edition.

luted water, but also worked on demonstrating the industrial sources, the factory-work hazards, of carbon monoxide poisoning and lead poisoning. As a result of her careful scientific studies, in 1919 Hamilton was appointed an assistant professor of industrial medicine at Harvard; she was the first female professor of any subject at Harvard, where she had a long and distinguished career.

A new spurt of environmentalism, one that has continued up to the present day and shows no sign of abating, began in the 1950s. It can perhaps be called universal environmentalism because it is now a value and ideological concern that moves so many people of so many different kinds and that is seen as relevant to so many different health and ecological problems. It is an environmentalism that was influenced by the post-World War II fears about radioactive fallout and its harmful consequences. And it was also influenced by the increasingly widespread knowledge among masses of now better-educated people of the harmful consequences not only of radioactivity but of many new chemicals and biological agents.

In the 1970s, distinguished biological scientists such as Professors Barry Commoner (*The Closing Circle*), the leader of the St. Louis Committee for Nuclear Information, and Paul Ehrlich (*The Population Bomb*), spoke out with great authority about the dangers of these problems to people's health and the world's ecology. They were listened to, but probably no one had more influence with communicating these problems than Rachel Carson, whose book, *The Silent Spring*, published in 1962, became an instant and continuing best-seller and has been translated into a dozen foreign languages.[18]

Carson's vivid description of the deadly effects of agricultural pesticides, particularly DDT, on human and animal life had a tremendous effect. Who could not envision what the lack of bird songs in the spring meant for unspoiled nature and its human and animal inhabitants? Carson called DDT and other chemical toxins "elixirs of death." Her extreme dictum was: "For the first time in the history of the world,

---

18. Originally published by Houghton Mifflin (Boston) in a regular trade edition, it has been kept in print continuously. Recently Houghton Mifflin (Boston, 1994) published a paperback twenty-fifth anniversary edition with an introduction by Vice President Al Gore.

every human being is now subjected to contact with dangerous chemicals from the moment of conception until death."[19]

Carson was a university-trained scientist who had worked for the government's Fish and Wildlife Service for sixteen years. She then retired to become a full-time writer as a result of success with her earlier books, such as *The Sea Around Us*. She filled *The Silent Spring* not only with scientific evidence but with the passionate rhetoric of her values and ideologies about an unspoiled natural world. There was some resistance to her book, of course, some ridicule, from spokespeople (counter-ideologists) from the chemical and food industries, and even from some scientists employed by these commercial interests. But Carson's work prevailed and has continued to have its continuing and powerful place in the world of current environmentalists.

As a result of her work and that of people like Ehrlich and Commoner, the world's first Earth Day was held in 1970; it is estimated that around 20 million Americans paraded and held rallies all around the country, perhaps most visibly in New York, Washington, D.C., and San Francisco. In 1992, World Summit Day, attended by delegates from around 150 countries, met in Rio de Janeiro to discuss environmental problems and possible solutions.

One of these current environmentalists, Vice President Gore, whose book was cited above, reports that he first read Carson's work at his mother's insistence, that it was discussed at the family dinner table, and that it had a "profound impact"[20] on him. He has made it one of his life's central moral passions and a continuing political and ideological concern.

In 1992, Gore, then still a senator, was present in Rio along with representatives of just about every other country in the world, at the United Nations Conference on Environment and Development, popularly known as the Earth Summit. They met to declare their universal environmentalist values and ideologies and to propose policies for dealing with such problems described by Gore as "the burning and clear-cutting of the tropical rain forests, the thousand-fold increase in

---

19. Carson, *Silent Spring*, 1962, 7.

20. Al Gore, *Earth in the Balance: Ecology and the Human Spirit* (Boston: Houghton Mifflin, 1992), 3.

the rate at which living species become extinct, the poisoning of our air and water, global warming and stratospheric ozone depletion—all these tragedies and more."[21] This "global environmental crisis," as it was called by the conference, was the rallying-point for the now universally defined environmentalism. Senator Gore speaks of "a family" of environmentalists facing this crisis.

But if the general values and ideologies of universal environmentalism are now here to stay, it has turned out that there are also specific points of difference among the different world regions, the individual countries, the different races and ethnic groups, the different genders, different economic classes, and those with different time perspectives.[22] Environmentalist values and ideologies now being both general and specific, it will often not be easy to accommodate and reconcile the differences. Environmentalism now speaks in many different voices.

The Development of the Market Ideology

In the analytical discussion of ideologies at the beginning of this chapter, I have emphasized that established ideologies are only more or less taken for granted. Of course, they are never perfectly stable even for their adherents; that is the case with all the components of the social system. And they are frequently, in some measure, challenged by one or another counter-ideology seeking to become the dominant, established view. Social systems are always in process; endless processes of reestablishment, development, and change are endemic in social systems. This is not to say that social systems are either random or chaotic; it is only to say that they are continually dynamic processes in which a considerable amount of stability, as well as development and change, can always be observed.

In this section, to examine some processes of development in ideologies, we look at the case of the development of the market ideology, which has now come to be the predominant, but not exclusive ideology

---

21. Gore, *Earth in Balance*, xii.

22. For an excellent set of case accounts of some of these specific ideological differences, see E. Melanie DuPuis and Peter Vandergeest, eds., *Creating the Countryside: The Politics of Rural and Environmental Discourse* (Philadelphia: Temple University Press, 1995).

in Western capitalist society and is also strong elsewhere around the world. As against the previous case of an ideology for a total society, this case provides an opportunity to examine an ideology for one of those major subsystems, in this case a social-structural subsystem rather than a cultural subsystem (that is, the economic or exchange system) that always exists in the larger, total social systems that we call societies. As we shall see, there seems to be a limited number of possible types of these economic or exchange systems and correspondingly a limited number of competing ideologies and counter-ideologies to legitimate and criticize the particular type that becomes established in the society. This case provides a further opportunity: to examine the relationship between ideology, which is a part of the culture of the social system, and the actual role and interaction systems that are a part of the social structure of the social system. Like all the major subsystems of the social system, the economic system concretely consists of an interaction between its social-structural components and some of the existing cultural components, of which ideology is always one. Sometimes it is development and change in the social structural component that occur first, with ideology following. That is the case with the market system of exchange and the market ideology. Sometimes, as with modern feminism, it seems to be the ideology that leads the way to change, with actual structures of gender roles and social interaction following on. The feminist "revolution" of recent times has been driven by powerful value and ideological statements.

In his seminal book, *The Great Transformation*,[23] Karl Polanyi, on the basis of extensive comparative historical study, proposed a valuable analytical typology consisting of three types of economic exchange: *reciprocal, redistributive,* and *market.*[24] The first type, the reciprocal form of economic or exchange system, occurs when the relevant values and norms either of a whole society or of some part of it prescribe that individuals who have reciprocal obligations to one another by virtue of their statuses in any one of a variety of particularistic collectivities— family, clan, tribe, fealty structures, friendships, or communities—give

---

23. New York: Farrar, 1944.

24. In this section I am following my article, "All Economies Are 'Embedded': The Career of a Concept, and Beyond," *Social Research* 62 (1995), 387–413.

to or receive from one another material or immaterial goods in traditionally patterned ways, just by virtue of those status relationships. Reciprocal exchange has been the predominant system of exchange throughout much of history and around the world, in civilized and primitive societies alike. Even in a predominantly market society such as exists in the modern world at the present, reciprocal exchange has an important role in gift exchange, which flourishes mightily alongside market exchange.[25]

Polanyi's second type of exchange, the redistributive, exists where values and norms prescribe that members of a collectivity—local, national, or even imperial—make contributions of taxes or goods or services to some central agency, primarily the government but also charitable organizations like the national Red Cross. This agency has the responsibility either of allocating these contributions to some collective enterprise of the collectivity, like defense or road construction, or of returning them in somewhat different measure and in somewhat different proportions to the original donors. Redistributive exchange can be seen in many relatively simple societies, as in the potlatch among the Northwest Coast Indians,[26] and of course it is enormously important in modern "welfare" societies like Sweden, but so it is also even in centers of capitalism like the United States, Great Britain, and Germany. All modern societies have defense, welfare, and other functions that are arranged chiefly on the basis of redistributive exchange.

Finally, the third of Polanyi's types is market exchange. In this type of exchange the values and norms prescribe that each and all of the partners in economic exchange must behave like rational man, like *homo economicus*, considering only price and not other obligations; buying cheap and selling dear; treating all buyers and sellers impersonally and honestly. While some market exchange existed at the margins in the great empires and societies of the past, it was never an honored activity; indeed, it was often carried on by despised or pariah internal groups or by merely tolerated foreign intermediaries. Since the late

---

25. For the best present theoretical and empirical sociology of gift exchange, see Viviana A. Zelizer, *The Social Meaning of Money* (New York: Basic Books, 1994).

26. A. Rosman and P.G. Rubel, *Feasting With Mine Enemy: Rank and Exchange Among Northwest Coast Societies* (New York: Columbia University Press, 1971. Reprinted, with new introduction, by Waveland Press, 1994).

eighteenth century, on the contrary, market exchange has grown proportionately ever greater in all the societies of the modern world and has become the admired and predominant form. It should be remembered, however, that in this modern world redistributive and reciprocal forms of exchange exist alongside market exchange.

In their time and place, each of these social structures has had, and continues to have, its legitimating ideology. But it is important to note that actual market exchange seems to have increased a great deal throughout the nineteenth century before it had a large and powerful ideology to support it. Indeed, in Great Britain, which was a central location for this growth of market exchange, aristocratic landowners spoke scornfully of those who were "in trade," and successful market-based manufacturers and bankers often sold out when they could afford to buy a landed estate where the principles of redistributive and reciprocal exchange were the honored forms, not the market. The owners of these estates might often be exploitative of their tenants and insufficiently paternalistic toward them, but they could nonetheless boast that they were not "in trade" any longer.[27]

The slow development of a positive ideology for the market can be seen in another way. Throughout the nineteenth century there is very little writing about the market as an emerging social-structural system. It is neither described for what it is nor praised for its important social functions and virtues. For example, even Adam Smith, the great progenitor of economic analysis, mentions the market in only one five-page chapter in his *Inquiry Into the Nature and Causes of the Wealth of Nations*. Marx similarly scanted the market. In the three-volume *Capital*, there is only one ten-page chapter on exchange and in that chapter the term "market" is used only twice, and then in passing. One last, striking piece of evidence for the neglect of the concept and ideology of the market: In the enormously detailed and immensely scholarly *History of Economic Analysis* (1954) by the great economist/social scientist theorist, Joseph Schumpeter, there is in its 1,200 pages no section on the market and the concept is not even listed in a subject index that is 30 pages long.

---

27. For this social process in eighteenth-century France, see Elinor G. Barber, *The Bourgeoisie in Eighteenth-Century France* (Princeton, NJ: Princeton University Press, 1955).

In sum, it would seem that the socio-historical process created the social structure of market exchange in a bits-and-pieces, incremental, unintended way. The theorists and ideologists who were actors in that process, likewise, created only theoretical and ideological bits-and-pieces of what gradually coalesced into a highly structured social scientific and ideological creation. Moreover, we must remember that developing ideologies are at first only counter-ideologies. Those who made these counter-ideologies justifying market values had to spend their energies criticizing the existing paradigms and ideologies that supported redistributive and reciprocal forms of exchange. Old theories and ideologies may die hard, sometimes in the face of massive change to new social-structural types of exchange. We may note that after the market ideology became predominant in the twentieth century, the redistributive proposals and ideologies of the Roosevelt era in America in the 1930s and the Beveridge welfare state proposals in post-World War II Great Britain had to struggle to be accepted.

But whatever their history, and that history certainly needs much more work than I have given it in this account,[28] the concept and ideology of the market are now predominant in modern western society.[29] The ideology stresses two values above all others, one being efficiency and the other freedom. Indeed, ideologies for the market often refer not to "the market" plain and simple but to "the free market" as if there could be some other kind. The phrase "laissez-faire" is another favorite ideological way of expressing the importance of freedom. And in the present movement toward reducing the redistributive efforts of current welfare arrangements and in recommendations and moves for "privatizing" government activities of many different kinds, the emphasis is on both values, freedom and efficiency. The ideological assertion is that the market can do almost anything the government does and do it more efficiently, at lower cost, and of course, with greater

---

28. For a valuable first step, see Richard Swedberg, "Markets as Social Structures," Working Paper No. 7, Department of Sociology, Stockholm University, 1993.

29. For a very sophisticated and witty discussion of the economics and ideology of the market in contemporary economic thought, see Donald N. McCloskey, *If You're So Smart: The Narrative of Economic Expertise* (University of Chicago Press, 1990), especially Chs. 10–11.

freedom for all. Where they exist at all, other ideologies are very much on the defensive. There is a diminished audience for the value of equity in this new ideological climate.

Making Everyday Ideologies

As I have emphasized throughout this chapter, because values and norms are ubiquitous in social systems, so also are the ideologies that support and criticize them. And the re-making and making anew of ideologies is also persistent and ubiquitous. In academic treatises, in books for the general public, in the mass media, in speeches, and in everyday life and conversation the confirming and making of ideologies is a constant process. In this section I want to look at this process as it occurs among ordinary people in everyday life.

Happily for this present purpose, some remarkably apt and excellent evidence is available in Professor William A. Gamson's book, *Talking Politics*.[30] Professor Gamson has been a long-standing and distinguished student of the sociology of social movements. Inevitably, since it is so often asserted that the mass media have an all-powerful effect on public opinion and thence on the creation and success or failure of social movements, Professor Gamson has become interested in the relationship of the mass media to social movements. He has become convinced that this relationship is usually described in oversimplified terms. More than the mass media is involved in the making of public opinion and of social movements. "Media discourse," he says, "is clearly not the only resource that most people use to construct meaning on political issues" (xi). His purpose is to understand "how it is that ordinary people sometimes do develop ways of understanding issues that support collective action for change" (xi). Note that Professor Gamson is interested in "ordinary people" and that he broadened out the problem of meaning-construction from "political issues" presumably to "issues" in general. Ordinary people do not merely "respond" to the meanings presented in the mass media; they are "thinking indi-

---

30. Cambridge, England: Cambridge University Press, 1992. As will become clear from our discussion, this excellent book should more accurately have been called *Talking Social Issues*.

viduals" who create meaning from the mass media and other sources. According to what Professor Gamson calls the three "central themes" of his book, people are neither "passive" nor "dumb" in the ways that they "negotiate" with the mass media to create meanings (4).[31]

What are some of the other sources and resources that people use to create everyday ideologies and other meanings for themselves? Professor Gamson mentions such things as "the experience of friends . . . as well as their own and others' work experience. They draw on shared subcultural knowledge and popular wisdom" about many social issues (4).

To explore his ideas, to test them empirically, Professor Gamson and his colleagues at Boston College undertook the very considerable research task of creating thirty-seven small groups, each with five members considered to be "ordinary people," to talk about a variety of current social problem issues, such as affirmative action, nuclear power, troubled industry, and Arab-Israeli conflict. The members of the group are described as "a broad and heterogeneous group of working people without higher education credentials and with only an average interest in public affairs" (10).[32] The discussions of these groups were recorded and analyzed to see if they confirmed Professor Gamson's several hypotheses about the actual processes of meaning formation by ordinary people. His book presents several of these recorded discussions and shows how they do indeed confirm the proposed hypotheses. I shall present, from the book, a typical one of these group discussions to illustrate my own hypothesis, that the making of everyday ideologies by ordinary people is indeed ubiquitous.

Professor Gamson's data are especially valuable for this purpose since, although he is actually describing the making of everyday ideologies, he never uses that term. "Ideology" is not listed in the book's index. Professor Gamson uses other language. He talks about how ordinary people construct "frames" of meaning; "frame" is the key con-

31. For extensive detailed discussion of these various ideological resources and the relationships among them, see Chs. 7–8.

32. See Ch. 2 for an excellent discussion of the suitability and limitations of the methodology of group conversations used in this research. "In sum," says Gamson, "the peer group conversations used here represent a hybrid form of social interaction: sociable public discourse among familiar acquaintances" (23).

cept. But it is clear that although there are cognitive elements in these frames, as there almost always are in all ideologies, they also have "values and norms" as an essential element, and those are of the essence of ideologies. In discussions of the different social problem issues, ordinary people express what Gamson calls a "strong injustice component,[33] one that breeds a sense of moral indignation" (4). As we shall see, in the discussion of affirmative action by a group of blacks, morally loaded terms and phrases like "institutional slavery, racism, and doors being slammed in one's face," all expressing a sense of felt injustice, (4) are used.

So Professor Gamson and his colleagues have been arduously busy recording everyday ideologies. Because they are primarily interested in how such ideologies might lead to collective action in social movements, we need to remind ourselves that ideologies may be as supportive of the existing social order as they sometimes are of changing it.

Here, then, is the book's report of one part of a group's discussion of affirmative action.

> *Place:* A home in Mattapan, a town in the greater Boston area. Five adults, all of them black, are seated in a circle in the living room. A tape recorder and a microphone rest on a table in their midst.
>
> *Time:* February, 1987.
>
> *Characters:* Aretha, in her thirties, a facilitator hired by researchers at Boston College; Vanessa Scott, in her forties, a teacher's aide; Mr. B., in his fifties, the owner of a small restaurant; Roy, in his twenties, a food service worker at a hospital; and Nicole, in her twenties, a manager at a fast food chain.
>
> *Aretha:* Another topic in the news is the issue of affirmative action—programs for blacks and other minorities. There's a disagreement over what kind of programs should we have, if any, to increase the hiring, the promotion, and the college admission of blacks and other minorities. When you think about the issue of affirmative action, what comes to mind?
>
> *Mr. B:* Ms. Scott, you always like to lead off. (*laughter in group*) I love listening to your voice.
>
> *Vanessa:* When I think about the issue of affirmative action, what comes

---

33. For a full discussion of the "injustice frame" as essential to social movements and the ideologies that may lead to them, see Gamson, *Talking Politics*, Ch. 2, "Injustice."

to mind? Well, basically, affirmative action, the affirmative action programs were instituted to redress past wrongs, right? All right. And I think that—was it in the, was [it] the sixties when Martin Luther King and his movement? (*nods from others*) Okay, I think that the gains that Martin Luther King made during that time have all been taken away. And now they've come out with this thing about what is it . . .

Roy: Reverse discrimination.

Vanessa: Reverse discrimination—meaning that because there were certain slots of certain programs allocated for black people to bring up the quotas in certain positions, and so on and so forth—it's discriminating against white people. But you have to understand that for centuries black people have been discriminated against, all right. And the only way you can redress that—redress that issue—is to set aside certain slots for black people or for minority people where they can at least, you know, be on par somewhat with the larger society. When I say larger society, I mean white people.

The way I see it now, all the gains that we have made and all the things that we have fought for have been taken away by your President Ronald Reagan. All right. And I see black people now going back to the time of slavery. Because that's what it—it's institutional slavery. I mean we're no longer—we don't have signs on doors that say "Black here and White here." We don't lynch black people anymore. But it's institutionalized. We go to get a job, we can't get it.

And now we can't even get into college anymore, because the Reagan administration has really—he has—what is—cut down on the—eliminated the financial aid, which makes it impossible for poor people and black people in particular, to even get into these institutions. Which means that if we cannot get the education, we cannot get the jobs. All right. So I see the doors being slammed in our faces again, and we're going back to the time of slavery.

Aretha: Any other—

Mr. B: Ms. Scott?

Aretha: —Mr. B?

Mr. B: It couldn't have been said no better.

Vanessa: Why, thank you.

Roy: I agree with Vanessa's views, too. 'Cause if you look at some of Reagan's appointments to the Supreme Court, for instance Chief Justice William—(*pause*); (*whispers*) Rehnquist.

Roy: Rehnquist—some of his views that—some of the things that he stood for—he was a very, I mean he is a very racist person. And I don't think he should have been nominated for the Chief Justice.

Vanessa: When you look at, you know, the Bakke decision. You know, this man brought charges that he was discriminated on the basis that

he was white because he could not get into a medical school. Okay—
and that because they have set aside certain slots for black people. And
when you read the information on this man—he was turned down
from five medical schools, not because he was white but because the
man was just not competent. Okay?

Nicole: Not qualified.

Vanessa: Well that was a whole turnaround, when that Bakke decision was
reached. That was the first time they brought a case about reverse
discrimination. How in the world can something be reversed when
we've been discriminated against all our lives? It cannot be reversed.

That is the conversation: not very sophisticated, in the everyday language of relatively uneducated people, but very definitely an ideology, that is, making a case for the values of justice and equality and a related case against their opposites. Gamson's book is full of examples of the way in which ordinary people make everyday ideologies. The conversation represents, in essence, a low- to middle-level example of culture, in this case in the area of ideology.

4

🌿 🌿 🌿

The Structure of Culture:
The "High" and "Low" Problem
and Intellectual Pursuits

I n this chapter we continue with the effort to improve our understanding of culture and intellectual pursuits by considering two
interrelated theoretical concerns. The first is the general and neglected matter of the *structure* of culture apart from its substance. The
second is the controversial matter of one aspect of cultural structure,
the "high"-"low" problem. Because it has been so controversial but is
of such great importance for understanding the nature of culture, we
deal with this problem at considerable length. The high-low problem
has been of great interest to intellectuals and sheds much light on the
nature of intellectual pursuits. With these purposes in view, this chapter provides extensive historical and contemporary illustration and
expansion of the analysis.[1]

---

1. For an earlier and somewhat different version of the matters treated in this
chapter, see Bernard Barber, "Is The Structure of Culture Hierarchical? The 'High
and Low' Problem," in Bernard Barber, *Constructing the Social System* (New Brunswick, NJ: Transaction Books, 1993), Ch. 16.

This article has an extensive critique of the "High and Low: Popular Culture
and Modern Art" show at the Museum Of Modern Art in 1990–1991. The curators of that show, Kirk Varnedoe and Adam Gopnik, in their extensive catalog
discussion of these matters have both an unsatisfactory definition of culture and

The Structure of Culture

As was described briefly in Chapter Two, culture—the system of symbols and ideas that exists in all social systems—is as much structured as is the inherent social structural components of such systems, including the kinship, political, economic, educational, and organizational structures. As I also pointed out in that discussion, the general confusion about the nature of culture is nowhere more clearly indicated than in the terminology that is used to refer to it. It is taken for granted in the terminology referring to the political, stratificational, kinship or other components of social structure that analysis of them must start with an account of their structure, however clear or unclear, however stable or changing that structure may be. But as to culture, the general problem of structure is seldom discussed, and the conventional terminology slides over this problem. Culture in general is seen as collections, sets, or what P.A. Sorokin liked to call "mere congeries" of symbols rather than as clear structures, that is, as relatively stable and recurrent patterns, sometimes hierarchical in nature, that are discerned in the endless process of action.

This blindness to the general problem of cultural structure is all the more striking and paradoxical in the light of the established analytical discussion of structure in all of the particular functional components of culture. For just one example, going back at least to ancient Greek society and certainly continuing right up to the present, the various types of structure of literature, that is, of such different types as prose and poetry and drama, have been at the center of sophisticated attention and scholarship. Music, too, and language and mathematics are cultural components of social systems that have long been analyzed in structural terms. In the modern world the structure of ideas in science has been intensively cultivated and, wherever possible, has been expressed in mathematical form. As the headline of a recent obituary in *The New York Times* for the distinguished physicist, Roman Smoluchowski, put it epigrammatically, "A life devoted to the mastery of structures from the atom to the planets." Or, as the biography of the

---

an unsatisfactory, unanalytical definition of "high and low." Their careful review of the existing literature concludes, correctly, that it is unsatisfactory, but they have nothing better to replace it.

Nobel Prize chemist, Linus Pauling, shows in great detail, his life's work was built on the discovery of the importance of structure for chemistry, not least of all with regard to the structure of protein, a line of work that was essential for the great discoveries eventually made in molecular biology.[2]

Progress in many of these specific areas of cultural scholarship is defined as any advance in the clarification and improvement of existing and changing structures. One of the major theoretical difficulties in the social sciences, and perhaps especially in sociology, is the lack of attention to structures, even in the area of social structure, but more so in the area of culture. We must remind ourselves that attention to structure does not mean necessary neglect of process or of instability and change in social systems. Indeed, process, instability, and change are inherent and continuous and can only be understood in relationship to structure. Process, change, and structure are just different aspects of action.

What is the reason for this lack of systematic general attention to cultural structure? One possible source is the view, again predominant in the social sciences, that "anything goes in culture," that culture is endlessly variable, endlessly alterable. There is a strong reformist and liberal spirit in the social sciences, a spirit that would like to have it that social systems are endlessly variable and endlessly alterable nearer the heart's desire. In the terms we have been developing up to now in this account of intellectual pursuits, it is assumed that much of the social sciences is inspired more by ideologies and their related values than by a passion for developing a mature science. And such a passion for and development of the social sciences as science would take the study of structures as a key focus. Where ideology and the passion for change prevail, structure is neglected, even derided and denied as the bulwark of conservatism and reaction.

The Hierarchical Structure of Culture: The "High" and "Low" Problem

In this chapter we will pay special attention to one aspect of the general problem of cultural structure. That aspect is the one that has come to

---

2. See the extremely interesting biography by Thomas Hager, *Force of Nature: The Life of Linus Pauling* (New York: Simon & Schuster, 1995).

be the much debated and quite controversial subject of the hierarchical, or high and low, structuring of culture, what I long ago referred to as the "hierarchy of knowledge" problem.[3] Before specifying and discussing the problem in detail, it is useful to point out that this debate and controversy has been especially prominent among a group of scholars and writers who refer to themselves as "the intellectuals." It is they who have created this as a "social problem," with too little explicit attention to it as a scientific problem.[4]

A word about the difference between a scientific problem and a social problem. A scientific problem is one that is defined by systematic theory and the relevant empirical data. A social problem is any condition of either the social structure or cultural structure of a social system that is defined by some group as morally bad, in need of elimination or alteration. It is usually necessary, first, to investigate as a scientific problem what is defined as a social problem to deal with it with some hope of effectiveness and success. That is the case for all social problems, such as poverty, crime, divorce, and, in the present case the social problem of the relation between high and low aspects of culture.

The social problem for many intellectuals, especially those specializing in literature, music, or the film, has been what they see as the emergence of what they call "mass culture," or "pop culture." Actually, popular culture in at least some small measure has existed for a long time and has only grown in size, public visibility, and command of resources as the population at large has become more educated after

---

3. On the importance of the middle level of the structures of culture, see the section below: Polarity or Range: The Importance of the the Middle Level of Culture.

4. As to the scarcity of scientific attention, I first dealt in a scientific-sociological way with what I called "the hierarchy of knowledge" problem in my paper, "Function, Variability, and Change in Ideological Systems," in Bernard Barber and Alex Inkeles, *Stability and Social Change* (Boston, MA: Little, Brown, 1971). Two other sociological analyses that tend to reject the existence of a hierarchy of knowledge, of high-low distinctions, are by Herbert Gans, *Popular Culture and High Culture: An Analysis and Evaluation of Taste* (New York: Basic Books, 1974); and Judith Blau, *The Shape of Culture*, Rose Monograph Series (Cambridge University Press, 1988). An excellent recent study of the Edinburgh arts festival by Wesley Monroe Shrum, Jr., shows the shortcomings of the Gans and Blau analyses. See Shrum, *Fringe and Fortune: The Role of Critics in High and Popular Art* (Princeton, NJ: Princeton University Press, 1996). See especially 6, 8.

the Second World War. It was then that some of the highly educated elites came to feel that the moderately educated masses cultivated literary, musical, and other forms of culture in a way that threatened their own elite ways. They have viewed it not only as a threat to the very substance and standards of their intellectual creations but also, in some degree, as a threat to their prestige, their resources, and their social influence. This alleged threat has been most loudly heard from intellectuals everywhere in the western world since World War II and perhaps especially from American intellectuals, because they have faced the most rapidly growing expansion of mass education and resulting mass culture anywhere in the Western industrial world. It is the purpose in this chapter to approach this high and low problem essentially as a scientific problem perhaps thereby to alter the understanding among intellectuals of how, and how much, it is a social problem.

The critical scientific fact about all the several types of idea and symbol systems that together make up the cultural structures of social systems is that they are subject to certain inherent dynamic internal and social processes that transform them in ways that make them harder to understand and control without special, sometimes lifetime, effort and devotion. Whether we look at scientific, philosophical, religious, or legal ideas; or musical ideas and symbols; the ideas of the graphic and plastic arts like painting, sculpture, and architecture; or ideas about language and mathematics, we discover that they are all capable of increasing degrees of abstractness (that is, degrees of generalization), systematization (that is, degrees of explicit connection with one another), and comprehensiveness with regard to subject foci (that is, degrees of coverage of the subject foci). Not only are they potentially capable of such dynamic processes, but they have all actually experienced such processes in considerable measure over the course of history, and often with increasing speed and volume in the modern world. Such processes are the focus of all science and scholarship.

Given the critical scientific fact of these dynamic processes in cultural systems, it is useful to refer to the different degrees of dynamic development in some clear way. Probably "more" and "less" would be vague and imprecise, but perhaps not so invidious in an egalitarian world as what has come to be the common usage, "higher" and "lower," terms that, of course, are also vague and imprecise. There is definitely a need here for a language of relative difference, of measurement, that would be clearly scientific and not judgmental and ideological. Some part of the controversy over high and low culture arises from the lack of understanding of its inherent dynamic processes, another from the lack of precise ways of talking about them.

These processes of cultural transformation have occurred in different measure in the several different cultural subsystems and also in the different social systems of the known world. It may be ventured, as a first approximation to what has happened in world history,[5] and just for rough illustration, that the cultural systems of religious ideas and philosophical ideas moved toward high levels of abstractness, systematization, and comprehensiveness first of all. Certainly, these cultural structures were highly developed in ancient China, Greece, and India. The same may be said for legal ideas in Roman society. Some scholars would say that prose and poetry, often combined with religious ideas, developed as high forms, discussed in abstract, systematic, and comprehensive terms, very early in ancient societies.

While there has always been considerable rational empirical knowledge (that is, embryonic science) of the physical, biological, and social worlds—human life is impossible without it—in even the simplest of human societies, and a good deal of it in the great ancient civilizations, it seems that higher forms of this kind of knowledge have developed only in the modern world, and there with increasing intensity and speed. "Science," the term for this higher and ever higher form of rational empirical knowledge of the physical, biological, and social worlds, is now the taken-for-granted term for this important intellectual pursuit. In the twentieth century there has even developed a specialized history of science that has done much to trace the emergence of this relatively late-developing, but now sometimes seemingly overwhelming form of higher culture.

Despite a great deal of outstanding scholarship, it is by no means settled among historians of science just why the modern higher form of science did not develop in earlier social systems or why it developed

---

5. I say "ventured" and "approximation" to emphasize that the following generalizations have been and should be the subject of intense scholarly study, not merely impressionistic views.

in different ways in different parts of the modern western world. It is also unsettled, of course, why biology developed later than physics and the social sciences last of all.

We should note an illuminating paradox. So much taken for granted is the development of modern science that no one refers to it as having higher and lower forms; there is no "pop science," though there is considerable effort to popularize it, that is, to make its higher form understandable in some way to those who are not scientists at all. Since it is now recognized that science is too important to the modern type of social system to be left only to the scientists, some understanding of science at "middle" and "lower" levels is now essential for members of the government, for citizens, and for those who educate them in schools and in the mass media. Science teachers and science journalists are now the essential middle-level (or, invidiously, "middle-brow") masters of scientific knowledge. They do more and less well in communicating the higher substance of science to the nonexpert public.

The Distribution of High and Low Culture and Some of Its Consequences

Culture, we have said, consists of ideas and symbols that are abstracted by the observer from social interaction. They may, at first glance, seem to exist primarily in the material products of social interaction: for example, in books and all other forms of printed materials, in musical compositions, paintings, sculpture, buildings and monuments, bridges and ships, machines, computers, and so forth. But these are all the creations of human interaction and so, ultimately, culture exists only in human minds. Some elements of culture probably exist in all minds—e.g., the knowledge that people cannot walk on water—but most cultural ideas and symbols are differentially and distributively located in some minds and not others. Many people have only, or chiefly, the lower forms of the ideas and symbols that are in their minds and actions. Some others add to this extensive lower content with various middle-level forms of some kinds of knowledge. And finally, some people add to this combination some higher culture that they have specialized in, that they have accumulated with considerable special training, effort, and continuous devotion. They are the active and creative scientists, scholars, musicians, theologians. They recognize one another as peers in a community of special, "advanced" knowledge. They speak to and write primarily for their peers.

Since specialized peers tend to address only others in their specialized cultural communities, there has emerged in recent years the problem of how these different communities can speak to one another. Scores of journals have emerged as "journals of opinion" in which different kinds of high-level peers can speak to one another. And now there has come into being a further problem: given the multiplicity of these journals of opinion, how can their readers speak to one another "across" these journals? Professor Daniel Bell of Harvard University has proposed a solution. Twice a year he will publish a "Newsletter of the Committee on Intellectual Correspondence" that will present thirty-two pages of summaries of and excerpts from such journals published in Europe, Japan, and the United States. This journal of journals will speak to cultural experts across cultural boundaries. The Newsletter is sponsored by the American Academy of Arts and Sciences in Cambridge, Mass., the Suntory Foundation of Japan, and the Institute for Advanced Studies in Berlin.

But these specialized cultural experts also may recognize a responsibility to transmit their advanced knowledge in a usable form to those at lower levels of understanding, especially to educators and journalists making a specialty in those fields of understanding science, or law, or art, or religion, or any other cultural area. Then, in turn perhaps, science, or law, or art, or religion, or any other cultural area in its established and newly emerging forms can be transmitted by these latter educators and journalists to those still lower down the hierarchy of knowledge. Each level of minds has its need and functions for the culture it possesses and often actively seeks.

Inevitably, among people located at the different levels of specialized cultural knowledge there is both admiration and some tension concerning one another. There is admiration because of the recognition of the talent and effort that goes into acquiring skill with ideas and symbols; there is admiration for what this achieved knowledge and its products contributes to the benefit and enjoyment of other actors and to the social system more generally. But there is some tension and resentment, too. Higher skill with ideas and symbols may sometimes be used, or be seen to be used, to the harm or degrading of others. For example, in the modern world, science and scientists are, on the whole, held in great admiration and richly supported with resources for their work. But there is also a strain of criticism, of complaint against these various cultural specialties. For example, science is blamed as the source of environmental destruction and deadly war. Or religious reporting is blamed for being too "secular." Intellectual battles, pro and con the various cultural fields, are the result. There is love and hate, admiration and criticism, praise and scorn, peace and war, among the different levels of the intellectual hierarchy. Both aspects of their relations are important in understanding all kinds of intellectual pursuits.

How "High" and "Low" Get Defined

Since culture is the product of intellectual creation, it follows that definitions of what is high, medium, or low in any given sphere of culture is also an intellectual creation. The establishing, legitimizing, and accepting of these definitions is often a complex matter, sometimes involving considerable and prolonged negotiation, tension, and conflict. Newly emerging cultural specialties are perhaps especially characterized by such complexities; they have to establish their claim to a higher form of intellectual substance. But the problem of definition of what is higher and lower may occur, as we shall see in a moment, even in well-established fields of the natural sciences.[6]

These complexities may occur both between disciplines and within disciplines. A recent controversy over Professor E. O. Wilson's highly abstract, systematic, and comprehensive theory of what he called "sociobiology"[7] is an example of conflicting definitions of scientific substance

---

6. For an illuminating discussion of some aspects of this problem, in papers analyzing what he calls processes of "boundary work," see Thomas F. Gieryn, "Boundary Work and the Demarcation of Science from Non-Science: Strains and Interests in Professional Identities of Scientists," *American Sociological Review*, 48(1983), 781–95; and Gieryn, "Boundaries of Science," in Sheila Jasanoff et al., eds., *Handbook of Science, Technology, and Society* (Thousand Oaks, CA: Sage, 1994).

7. Wilson, *Sociobiology: The New Synthesis* (Cambridge, MA: Harvard University Press, 1971).

between disciplines at the highest levels of theory. Professor Wilson offered his "new synthesis" as a biological theory explaining all behavior, by insects, animals, and humans alike, in the same biological terms. Since the social sciences are based on a different abstract, systematic, and comprehensive theory of behavior, namely, that such behavior consists of "action," not biological phenomena, of meanings not physiological phenomena, there was a great critical outcry from the social sciences. Sociobiology was denounced as a reductionist theory, incompatible with the established and fundamental social science theoretical assumption about human behavior.[8] The furor has died down over the last twenty years, but there has been no resolution of this quarrel between Wilson, some of his supporters, and even a few supporters from the social sciences, on the one side, and the great mass of the social scientists who go their own established way, on the other. For now, the two disciplines go their own way pretty much; whether there will be some new resolution of this high theoretical difference in the future remains to be seen. That is the way in the sciences. For now there is no authoritative peer group to rule one way or the other.

Functions of and Limits of Peer Review

Within disciplines and cultural specialties, the primary mechanism for making decisions about what scientific discovery, or new scholarship, or "original" painting or music, or other cultural creations are higher and lower is peer review (or what is called in some fields a jury of experts). Peers and experts are those who are established as the existing creators and maintainers of the recognized body of the higher standards and substance in the given field.[9] There are many particular and

---

8. Among a plethora of works arguing the essentiality of this assumption, still a classic is Talcott Parsons, *The Structure of Social Action* (New York: American Book Company, 1937).

9. For evidence on this point from the field of late-twentieth-century architecture, see Magali Sarfatti Larson, *Behind the Post-Modern Facade: Architectural Change in Late Twentieth Century America*, (Berkeley, CA: University of California Press, 1993), especially Ch. Four. See also, Robert Venturi, *Iconography and Electronics Upon A Generic Architecture: A View From the Drafting Room* (Cambridge, MA: M.I.T. Press, 1996).

some general criticisms of the peer review system, but on the whole, almost always after intensive scrutiny of its functions and processes, it is judged, like democracy among types of government, as the "least bad" system for making its often difficult decisions.

Inevitably, because of the esoteric knowledge that is at issue in every special field, the creation of peer review committees and expert juries is left to the organizational arrangements set up by the official representative bodies of each field. Granting agencies and review journals appoint expert peers to judge the various claims made by scientists and other intellectuals, creators of other kinds of culture. It is their task to make awards of resources, prizes, and prestige on the basis of their evaluations of the relative likelihood that different applicants and claimants have already made or are likely to make contributions to the advancement of higher forms of the cultural specialty in which they are expert. There seems to be no specialty in which there is not some grumbling and protest against the decisions of particular peer review committees. Mostly this protest is informal, but sometimes it makes formal protest to the official specialty body that has set up the peer review committee that has been alleged to be guilty of gross error or malfeasance. In some cases though, the disputes about expertise and about what is higher and lower come into the governmental judicial system as we shall see in the next section.

Peer Review and Expertise in the Courts

A brief history of how the American courts have treated the matter of peer review and expert testimony illuminates the general difficulty and complexity of these processes.[10] The American courts have always had to deal with some matters of disputed expert evidentiary testimony, but the scope, magnitude, and intensity of these disputes has increased greatly during the twentieth century with the great increase in higher scientific knowledge and esoteric technology. Courts have differed as

---

10. For this account, I am very much indebted to Shana M. Solomon and Edward J. Hackett, "Setting Boundaries Between Science and Law: Lessons From *Daubert v. Merrell Dow Pharmaceuticals, Inc.*," *Science, Technology, & Human Values*, 21 (1996), 131–156.

to their standards for judging those alleged experts who have been offered by both sides to a court proceeding as having higher knowledge to offer as evidence.

As they will, given the law's need for an acceptable amount of certainty and consistency, judges in different courts looked for some standardization, and they finally found it in what was called the Frye Rule after a 1923 decision by the District of Columbia Circuit Court concerning the admission of evidence from the then-new polygraph, or lie detector, machine. The essence of the Frye Rule, Solomon and Hackett say, was that the polygraph machine "had not yet gained such standard and scientific recognition among physiological and psychological authorities" that it could be admitted into evidence. This Frye Rule was known as the "general acceptance rule."

But there was soon difficulty in knowing just what "general acceptance" meant. Did it mean acceptance by all who claimed to have the higher or expert knowledge, or only a majority of them, or only a plurality, or just a significant minority? Congress tried to come to the aid of the courts in the 1975 version of the *Federal Rules of Evidence*. Rule 702 lowers the Frye Rule standard by stating: "If scientific, technical, or other specialized knowledge will assist the trier of fact to understand the evidence or to determine a fact in issue, a witness qualified as an expert by knowledge, skill, experience, training or education may testify thereto in the form of an opinion or otherwise." This rule has been called "the helpfulness rule" or "the relevancy rule." But it too was unsatisfactory; some critics said it allowed for the admission of "junk science."

Finally, as a result of much disagreement in the lower courts, in 1993 the Supreme Court handed down a decision in the case of *Daubert v. Merrell Dow* that was intended to clarify issues and eliminate future disagreement. But it seems not to have succeeded. The Court's best efforts resulted only in illuminating the complexity of the higher-lower determination problem and left the lower courts only with a set of guidelines that are still not easy to apply to specific cases.

For its decision, which was only four pages long and therefore looked simple, but was not, the Court had the weighty assistance of twenty-one amicus curiae (friend of the court) briefs. Of course the pharmaceutical manufacturers weighed in, but so also did the established national natural science associations like the American Association for the Advancement of Science and the National Academy of Sciences, the most prestigious medical journals such as *The New England Journal of Medicine*, groups of law professors with special knowledge and interests in the issues, working scientists, and cooperating groups of historians, philosophers, and sociologists of science (on both sides of the issue). From all this advice, the Court was assured of a full panoply of views to consider.

The Court began by stating that "many factors will bear on" the inquiry into relative expertise and higher and lower knowledge in any particular case coming before a court. They laid out the four following considerations for a court to take into account in making decisions, but insisted that these were not a final checklist or test but only "observations" that trial judges should keep in mind.

1. Falsifiability: Is the hypothesis testable? This consideration showed that the Court had listened to the amicus curiae briefs that contained discussions of scientific methodology. In his dissent from the majority opinion, Chief Justice Rehnquist opined that he did not think many trial judges would know what falsifiability meant.

2. Peer review and publication. The Court held that peer review is important, but having heard about the limitations of peer review from the amicus brief of some sociologists of science, it held that peer review was "relevant, though not dispositive."

3. Known or potential rate of error and the existence and maintenance of standards in the research knowledge claims of the contending parties.

4. General acceptance. This seems a throwback to the Frye Rule, which the Court had rejected, but nevertheless the Court held that it could still be relevant. However, like its predecessors, the Court did not specify how general acceptance was to be determined. Thus, the lower courts are left with a set of "observations" that are probably something of an improvement on both the Frye Rule and Rule 702 but that obviously leave them with plenty of deciding to do.

The four observations have come to be known as the *Daubert* Factors but they are clearly not a simple measurement or decisional instrument.[11] In Chief Justice Rehnquist's summary dissenting words, the four factors are "not only general, but vague and abstract." This is harsh and not quite accurate, but clearly social science is left with the problem of improving distinctions of higher and lower both in regard to culture in general and also in the several particular cultural areas. We are left with the conclusion that what is difficult and complex even in science and even with the measured reasonableness of the courts, is even more so in other cultural areas.

Alternatives to Peer Review: Power, Income, Class, Ideology

But not all venues provide the relatively measured reasonableness of the courts. In a society like ours, where there are considerable differences in class, income, ideology, and political power, these differences may affect the determination of what is higher or lower at some times, in some cultural area. These differences may override the genuine substance of the cultural stuff in question. Thus, holders of higher income or greater power may decree that one type of art or music is to be considered higher than another against the contrary views of the art or music experts. Income or power may be wedded to the traditional forms, which once may have been the higher but have now been either exceeded or equaled by new work. There are lags as well as continua, therefore, in the dynamic processes of cultural systems. As I pointed out earlier, even in science there has been some resistance by established scientists to discoveries of new and improved forms of knowledge. The classic case in science was the resistance to Mendel's discovery of the particulate character of the components of the human organism and of the other species of fauna and flora.[12]

---

11. For one very careful and deliberate attempt to use the *Daubert* case factors and recommendations, see *Science*, January 3, 1997, 21. In this attempt, a federal judge in Oregon, presiding over a case having to do with alleged harms to women from silicone-gel breast implants, made intensive use of expert peer review panels to evaluate the scheduled testimony of a whole series of experts for the plaintiffs and the defendants. As a result of the panels' work, the judge ruled out all claimed expert testimony.

12. See Bernard Barber, "Resistance by Scientists to Scientific Discovery," *Science* 136 (1961), 596–602.

The Patron Problem

Because of such other important differences as income, ideology, and power, some cultural areas are confused, when distinctions of high and lower are being made, by what can be called "the patron problem."[13] In regard to science, resources come from patrons such as the foundations and government who make their decisions about higher and lower by using peer review and expert groups. In the graphic arts, music, and dance, however, wealthy patrons may make decisions themselves, making their own decisions about what is to be considered higher. The history of art is filled with examples of faulty, as well as excellent, decisions by wealthy patrons. Art museums have been, and perhaps continue to be, stuffed with both their wise choices and their mistakes. Expert curators now function to some extent, as art dealers did in the past, as safeguards against some willful and, as it is eventually seen, mistaken patrons, but curators may still bend before the power, prestige, and income of some patrons.

The Role of New Technology and Knowledge

A further element of systemic confusion is introduced into decisions about higher and lower forms of culture by the great and rapid increase in our times of new technology, specialized knowledge, intensive interest, and devoted expertise in many cultural areas. We may take the two instances of photography and jazz music as illustrative examples, which we treat in turn. As we shall note, while there is now much expert attention to, and critique and history of, photography, the comparable treatment of jazz is very much larger. As one member of a music conservatory faculty recently remarked casually, "Jazz is now the American music." This definition has called forth not only widespread apprecia-

---

13. For a recent report on the patterns and problems of present-day patronage in the fields of the performing arts in the United States, with a special emphasis on the situation in New York City, the national center for the performing arts, see Judith Miller, "As Patrons Age, Future of Arts is Uncertain," *The New York Times*, Feb. 12, 1996, A1, C12. For further information on patterns and motivations for giving by patrons, see Francie Ostrower, *Why The Wealthy Give* (Princeton, NJ: Princeton University Press, 1995).

tion of and devotion to jazz at popular and "higher" intellectual levels, it has also produced a massive body of scholarship.

From Low to High: The Case of Photography

First, then, for the emergence of photography as a higher art. The technology of photography has existed for almost one hundred and fifty years. That technology has improved continuously and rapidly, so that by now almost everyone and anyone, child or adult, can "point and shoot" and take pictures.

For a long time, and still to a great extent, there has not been much art, not much higher knowledge, among those who take pictures, of its artistic possibilities. As the sociologist Pierre Bourdieu and his colleagues showed by their several studies in France during the 1960s, most photographs have always been, and still are, routine shots of family events like weddings, birthdays, other family gatherings, and vacation events and places.[14] Hence their description of photography as a "middle-brow art." As late as the sixties, one set of subjects in Bourdieu's studies expressed interest in photography as a "higher" art form but were uncertain about their views and their social situation as aspirants to "higher" forms for photography. As Bourdieu's colleague, Jean-Claude Chamboredon, put it: "Photographic aesthetes are clearly aware of the social situation of their art. When they denounce the ambiguous cultural status of photography they are naming the true source of their anxiety."[15]

In contrast, in the United States, where most photography is still also a middlebrow art or even lower, photography as a high art form emerged early in this century and flourished as such in specialized photographic galleries and among experts devoted to demonstrating their claims to creating a high art.[16] Photography as high art was perhaps

---

14. See *Photography: A Middle-brow Art* (Palo Alto: Stanford University Press, 1996). This is, of course, a translation and re-publication of the 1960s work.

15. Ibid., 149.

16. For a brilliant if condensed critical history of American photography from the Civil War to the present, based in considerable measure on the twenty-five books listed in its bibliography, see Luc Sante, "American Photography's Golden

only most clearly established and legitimated by the Museum of Modern Art when it set up a photography department in the 1940s with its own expert curator and held special exhibits to demonstrate its conviction that photography had as much claim to being a higher art as painting or sculpture.

This difference between France and the United States with regard to photography is an example of the fact that higher forms of old and new art may appear at different times in different societies. Variable historical and sociological circumstance play their part in the emergence of the higher forms of the various areas of culture. For example, France may have been a laggard with regard to photography, but it was certainly not a laggard with regard to painting, where it was among the first in the western industrial world all during modern times. France, as we shall also see in the discussion of jazz, was no laggard in that cultural area either.

From Low to High: The Case of Jazz

Jazz has sometimes been called the "New Orleans music."[17] Originally a hybrid of African instrumental music and European styles of music, jazz emerged in New Orleans around the turn of the twentieth century. Why New Orleans? There were a number of special historical and social circumstance in the New Orleans situation. Since New Orleans was a much more Europeanized urban place than the rest of the rural, race-segregated, formerly slave-holding South in which it was

---

Age," *The New York Review of Books*, April 4, 1996, 62–67. Sante is a fine example of the cultural expert who applies his higher standards and higher knowledge to discuss the higher and other levels of a cultural area.

17. The following account of the transformation of jazz from a lower to a higher form of musical art, is very much indebted to a briefing paper prepared for me by Professor Robert Lyons of the Queens College, C.U.N.Y., English Department and Program on American Studies. Professor Lyons has been for almost forty years a connoisseur, scholar, and teacher of the social history of American jazz.

For some very detailed history of the transformation of jazz in America, see James Lincoln Collier, *The History of Jazz* (New York: Delta, 1978); and Collier, "The History of Jazz," in Barry Kernfeld, ed., *The Grove Dictionary of Jazz* (New York: St. Martin's Press, 1988).

located, some of its later-nineteenth century black popular musicians were aware of and had access to European musical styles as carried on by its remaining French and Creole populations. The hybrid music, not yet jazz, that was created became very familiar in American music in the late nineteenth century, in part through church music; in part through vaudeville entertainment (especially in the widely popular minstrel shows); in part through the blues tradition[18] that emerged from Southern country traditions; and finally, in part through early black syncopated musical traditions that prevailed in lower-class entertainment sites. Such sites were supported by the established social structure of New Orleans in the form of sporting clubs, brothels, saloons, and dance halls. Such places flourished in New Orleans's Storyville District, its red-light, honky-tonk area that was closed down only after the United States declared war in 1917 and New Orleans became a port of embarkation for American troops going to Europe. Storyville was the New Orleans equivalent of New York's Tenderloin District, which did not, however, support the emerging jazz music.

Jazz bands, as such, probably emerged out of the existing marching bands that were popular in the later nineteenth and early twentieth centuries. Dating is difficult because of the absence of contemporary recordings, but by 1915 there were probably specialized jazz bands playing the syncopated music that was the hallmark of jazz. The first King Oliver-Louis Armstrong recordings that were made in 1923 indicate that New Orleans-style jazz was already firmly established.

A common assumption in the historical literature is that some of the creole musicians who possessed some formal musical training, and therefore familiarity with European musical styles, became interested in the rougher music of the blacks and turned it in the jazz direction. However, more likely, these early musicians had only limited formal training, and anyway, most of the music was played by ear, and arrangements were still primitive at this time. Jazz was not yet independent. The New Orleans bands had to play for their popular white audiences a mixture of European music such as waltzes, quadrilles, rag-

---

18. On the special character and history of blues music, and its long-continuing relationship with and effects on other forms of jazz, see Paul Trynka, *Portrait of the Blues* (London: Hamlyn, 1996). For a brief account, see "The Rebirth of the Blues," *The Economist*, May 4, 1996, 87–88.

time, and popular songs when they were in white venues; at black pic-
nics, funerals, parades, and dances, they could play more jazz. The
bands could earn a living only by catering to this variety of musical
taste and knowledge.

While still appealing to lower and middle cultural tastes, during and
after World War I jazz migrated vigorously out of New Orleans. First,
during that time, many African-Americans went north to work in the
cities and carried the new music with them. Large numbers went to
Chicago, which became the new jazz center. Chicago's South Side was
a wide-open district for all-night dance halls, saloons, and associated
amusement centers that employed large numbers of musicians.

Secondly, white musicians in the Northern cities developed an interest in jazz. In Chicago such soon-to-be-celebrated white musicians as
Benny Goodman and Eddie Condon came to this music by hearing it
on Chicago's South Side. The white musicians were young and attracted to this new "hot" music despite its being considered disreputa-
ble by their elders and mentors. New York, Los Angeles, and Chicago
developed special jazz communities that recognized its commercial
possibilities for the dance craze that developed among young whites
generally during the 1920s.

Finally, the new technology of recorded music and phonographs
spread the musical appreciation of jazz. Recordings of jazz music had
begun in 1917 with a series of records made by the Original Dixieland
Jazz Band, a group of white musicians who copied the music they heard
in New Orleans.[19] Through records, jazz was disseminated to many
listeners and would-be musicians. During the '20s and '30s the major
record companies discriminated against black musicians and bands, but
distributed these "race records," as they called them, primarily in the
black community. Jazz still had a lower cultural status.

This status began to move up in the '20s, sometimes called the Jazz
Age because jazz seemed to symbolize the more modern, progressive,
energetic, and liberated post–World War I American culture. Speak-
easies, nightclubs, and cabarets became identified with the new youthfulness of America. They were the expressions of a more permissive
society that now welcomed more sexual freedom and less inhibition in

---

19. One of the first of these records is "Livery Stable Blues."

speech and musical expression. Jazz was made for this new cultural atmosphere and helped to advance it.

Intimate couple-dancing, as against the older prim Victorian group-dancing, essentially embodied the new individualistic expressiveness. Nightclubs and commercial ballrooms such as the legendary Roseland Ballroom in New York City became important locales for the new dancing. Roseland, which opened in 1919, began in 1924 to feature all-black bands, still playing, of course, for white dancers only. The Savoy Ballroom in Harlem became the counterpart to Roseland; adventurous young whites looking for excitement thought it was a great thing to go to the Savoy and dance with the black dollar-a-dance women. Everywhere, the black jazz bands became popular because a rhythmic jazz style had become associated with youthfulness, excitement, and unconventionality. Many Hollywood films of the time—for example, those featuring such actresses as Clara Bow and other examples of the flapper type—enhanced this new cultural image.

One result of this new appreciation for jazz was the decline of the small black jazz band and the emergence of the so-called big band, appealing to a national and mass radio audience. In these bands jazz music began to require schooled musicians who could read and execute written scores. It required composers/arrangers with formal training and compositional talent. Playing by ear decreased and the big bands became the musical educators for those with limited formal training. Charlie Parker, from Kansas City (Missouri, though born in Kansas City, Kansas) who became a major jazz innovator, developed his remarkable talent through apprenticeship with the new big bands. By starting with the big bands, more blacks from the middle class and with some formal training, became professional jazz musicians. In this category belong such distinguished blacks who eventually had bands of their own as Duke Ellington, Fletcher Henderson, and Jimmy Lunceford.

Another consequence of the big bands' success was the increased merging of the lower jazz music with the more approved higher forms. Paul Whiteman, a white man, who billed himself as "the King of Jazz" in the 1920s, introduced a string section into his big band. He played elaborately orchestrated versions of popular songs in what he called "symphonic jazz." He sought to improve the social if not the musical status of his kind of jazz by giving concerts apart from dance halls and clubs. He was immensely popular with his middle-level audiences at the time, but the hybrid he created is now discredited and jazz highbrows do not listen to his records.

In the late 1920s jazz attracted the attention and devotion of three groups that finally established a secure higher cultural status for it. The first was a group of New York intellectuals who encouraged and celebrated the higher black culture in general, not only jazz, but its fiction, poetry, drama, and graphic arts in what is now known as the Harlem Renaissance.[20] Such members of the Harlem Renaissance group itself as the poet Langston Hughes experimented with jazz rhythms in his poetry.

A second group, to some extent influenced by the first one, consisted of college students who responded to jazz as twentieth-century music much as they began to define film as a new twentieth-century high art. These students encouraged the performance of both films and jazz on their campuses. Strange now to think of these two art forms as new.

Third, some groups in Europe, especially in Paris, became aware of jazz through the medium of touring American jazz bands. But jazz in Europe was never so important as it was in the United States.

All of these three groups wrote appreciative essays about jazz in magazines for educated readers. Books followed the essays. The first books on jazz came in the early '30s from Europe by the Belgian Robert Goffen and the French Hugues Parnassie. Neither is considered seminal today, but they gave the first broad overview of jazz as serious high art. And some of the college students whose interest had been aroused in the '20s, men like Marshall Stearns (Harvard) and John Hammond (Yale) became the jazz record producers, reviewers, and essayists of the next decade. In the 1930s, as a clear sign of the rise to higher art status of jazz, specialized journals devoted to jazz news and

---

20. One of these intellectuals was the general cultural critic Gilbert Seldes. See his biography in Michael Kammen, *The Lively Arts: Gilbert Seldes and the Transformation of Cultural Criticism* (New York: Oxford University Press, 1996). And see also the informative review of this book by Arthur M. Schlesinger, Jr., *The New York Times*, Book Review Section, May 5, 1996.

criticism were founded, *Downbeat* in 1934 and *Metronome* in 1939. These were read in highbrow, avant-garde circles.

The 1930s were a time of prosperity and ever higher cultural status for jazz. It now became separated from its low origins in dives and brothels, though it continued to have a life there, too. Outstanding jazz musicians such as Benny Goodman, Jimmy and Tommy Dorsey, and Artie Shaw, all white men, enjoyed national renown and popularity. But black jazz musicians like Duke Ellington and Count Basie also became widely known and appreciated for their high art. The music industry now distributed its jazz records across the race groups. The high cultural status of jazz was demonstrated by concerts in the prestigious classical music halls such as Carnegie Hall in New York and similar ones in the other leading cities.

Another sign of the continuing high seriousness of jazz was the emergence in the post–World War II period of protest by some jazz musicians against the earlier established forms. They wanted to continue creating and introducing innovations and were content to present their efforts to those who truly appreciated them and their aspirations. A result was the resurrection of small jazz clubs where the creative players and the expert audiences could carry on. These jazz advances were noticed in special journals that now had a definite general musicological thrust. Jazz became more of a special music for a special audience, just like classical music. It is a mark of achievement of higher cultural status in any area when there appear some differences at the forefront of its creative community; jazz has attained that mark.

But such a community needs training, resources, and moral support. In postwar American society, these have come to jazz. Beginning in the 1960s, the established musical training institutions such as the New England Conservatory in Boston and the Juilliard School in New York, which is now a part of Lincoln Center for the Performing Arts, set up curricula for jazz music that were coequal with classical curricula. Jazz had, in effect, also become classical. Finally, in 1995, Lincoln Center set up an independent Jazz Center to become the equal of its other higher performing art forms: classical symphonic music, chamber music, opera, ballet, theater, and film. There are now a Jazz Orchestra, a regular jazz season (beginning in 1996–97), and jazz festivals, all headed up by a nationally distinguished black musical performer and teacher, Wynton Marsalis, who is trained in both classical and jazz music. Marsalis is designated the artistic director of the Jazz Center just as James Levine is the artistic director of the Metropolitan Opera. The migration of jazz from New Orleans to the world's capitals as a higher form of art was now complete.

But also, just as in the case of other kinds of the higher art forms, a middlebrow style of jazz, known as smooth jazz, now flourishes. It is described as "radio's hottest format"[21] today, played much more widely than higher jazz, and selling far more records. Paradoxically, it may be a sign that a set of cultural forms and ideas has achieved a higher status, appreciated by experts describing it in general, systematic, and comprehensive terms, when that set has also produced a middle level status scorned by the experts. That is now the case for jazz.

Struggling to Rise: The Case of Crafts

I have stressed that there is a dynamic in every cultural area that impels those who cultivate its substance and those who devote themselves to appreciating its products to strive to take it to higher levels of abstractness, systematization, and comprehensiveness, in short, to make it a recognized, accepted part of high culture along with science, painting, music, and the other cultural systems that already reside there. As we have seen, in very recent times photography and jazz have striven successfully. How about the loosely defined and very variegated category of creative activities lumped under the vague term "crafts"? It is a category that includes such activities, among others, as weaving (rugs and tapestries), metalsmithing (especially of gold objects), pottery and ceramics, glass-making, furniture, jewelry, and basketry. For some of these, like weaving, goldsmithing, and pottery, claims by some makers and appreciators for higher artistic status have been made for centu-

---

21. For an informative article on smooth jazz, see Tom Masland and Yahlin Chang, "Jazz For Drive Time. Muzak With a Backbeat? It's Radio's Hottest Format," *Newsweek*, May 20, 1996, 76.

ries.[22] For the others, the recent past has seen a great efflorescence, certainly in the United States, of craft-making and craft-connoisseurship. Craft fairs, sometimes juried, at which craft objects of all kinds and qualities are displayed and sold to large crowds, are held all around the country and at nearly all seasons of the year. Some fairs, those most likely to be juried and presumably selective, are under the sponsorship of the American Crafts Council, a national organization striving to improve the quality and appreciation of crafts. There now exist some schools and studios, like the Rhode Island School of Design and Dale Chihuly's glass studio in Seattle, Wash., specializing in training their students for high art in their fields. Journals are published and there is even an American Craft Museum in New York City right across the street from the Museum of Modern Art, and also an American Museum of Folk Art right across the street from the Lincoln Center for the Performing Arts. But in neither of these two bastions of high art are crafts or their museums accepted the way film and jazz now are.

It is clear that there are elements in the crafts world that are struggling to define themselves and be defined by others as high art. But the Lincoln Center and other parts of the American high art world do not so define them.[23] *The New York Times* does not give craft activities continued and systematic attention, it does not have a special editor or editors for crafts the way it does for science, music, jazz, and other fields of established high culture. Crafts are treated only sporadically.

In Britain, in contrast, perhaps because of the large and continuing admiration for the work of William Morris, at least one influential

---

22. As an example, a hundred years ago the "eminent Victorian," William Morris, developed and sought a high art status for a whole list of crafts: engraving, book design, calligraphy, embroidery, furniture, stained glass, textiles, tapestries, wallpaper, and murals. See Michael Kimmelman, "A Master Best Known For His Chair," *The New York Times*, May 24, 1996, C1, C17. Perhaps it is a sign of the fact that crafts are now defined as high art in some quarters that the author of this article, Kimmelman, is the Chief Art Critic of *The Times* and the article is published under the head, "Art Review." See also the monumental biography by Fiona MacCarthy, *William Morris: A Life For Our Time* (New York: Knopf, 1995).

23. There are exceptions. For example, the Brooklyn Museum of Art has featured for a whole year the glass art creations of Dale Chihuly on its entrance atrium wall. And Chihuly has recently had a show in one of the established art galleries in New York's Soho.

journal has spoken of crafts as art. *The Economist*,[24] speaking of a recent show in London of Morris's work, says, "An art show? Yes, for that is where the show ends, and in Britain at least craft is moving at great speed in that direction. Forget the 1930s ceramicist's bowls or bottles; studio ceramics today is rapidly becoming sculpture. Studio glass too is becoming an art form. So are textiles and much else."

Why are crafts not yet recognized, as certainly in part they might be, as high art? Is it because the vast majority of craft products are still defined by the relevant experts as only of low or middle rank as artistic creations? Is it because this mediocre and highly variegated mass swamps and conceals the specialized higher creations? Is it because there is still, in addition to the striving for high art status in the craft world, a very strong anti-hierarchical ideology that the making of crafts is just folk art, an everyday activity requiring no special knowledge or devotion? We can only speculate on this interesting matter and hope that some serious study of the makers and consumers of craft products will be forthcoming in the future.

Is "Primitive" Art High or Low?

Asking this question, a question that is often debated, provides us an opportunity to state again the main argument of the discussion of that aspect of the structure of cultural systems that we call the high and low problem. The argument is that a scientific analysis of this problem holds that elements of a cultural system become high when they become the focal objects of generalized, systematic, and relatively comprehensive analysis and evaluation by a group of knowledgeable, committed experts who have specialized in the study of the relevant cultural system. There is nothing intrinsic to a cultural system, to any cultural idea, symbol, or meaningful artifact that establishes it as low, medium, or high. Such establishment is always the product of the relevant group of experts.

Thus, before its "discovery," before it became the object of close attention by scholars of western and world art and was defined by them

---

24. June 1–7, 1996, 84.

as worthy of systematic, generalized, comprehensive analysis and evaluation, the primitive art produced by non-literate societies around the world was treated not as art but as meaningful ritual objects by the members of the societies that created them. However, for about a hundred years or more now, a great many, but not all of these objects have been transformed by such expert attention and evaluation into high art.

Noted at first by a few maverick connoisseurs and collectors, then taken up by brilliant avant-garde painters and sculptors in the School of Paris as worthy of study and emulation, and finally given intensive study and high evaluation by many members of the community of expert art scholars, what were originally particularistic ritual objects have now been transformed into objects of generalized artistic significance. This significance is expressed not only in scholarly study but also by the collection of high primitive art in both general and special art museums and art exhibitions around the western world. In New York, for example, the Metropolitan Museum of Art has extensive collections of art from primitive societies from around the world. In the 1980s, at a show on Primitivism at the Museum of Modern Art co-curated by William Rubin and Kirk Varnedoe, these curators explored the nature and functions of primitive art and its complex relations with high modern art. This show was followed in 1990–1991 by a show co-curated by Varnedoe and Adam Gopnik called "High and Low: Popular Culture and Modern Art," which had important bearing on the subject of the earlier show.[25] There has also been in New York, for some twenty years or so, a special museum, the African Art Museum, which displays past and current African art that experts writing about the Museum's exhibitions have evaluated as low, medium, and high in diverse measure. And, to take one further example, the Guggenheim Museum in 1996 has sponsored another blockbuster show of high primitive art from nearly all quarters of the African continent. As it has entered the world of art in general, and become subject to the evaluation of experts, primitive art is judged by the same standards as all other kinds of established art and thereby has been evaluated as low, medium, or high in quality. As with all cultural systems, expert standards now prevail for

---

25. On this latter show, see my critical comments in footnote 1 above.

primitive art, not just adventitious intrinsic characteristics. Primitive art can now be either high or mass-produced "airport art" sold to nonexpert tourists as souvenirs rather than as art objects.

High-Middle-Low Communication and the Processes of Democracy

Viewed as a whole, the cultural system of a society consists of a mixture of high, middle, and low subsystems of ideas and symbols. The mixture of the three levels of cultural cognitive ideas, symbolic elements, and moral statements may vary over time and among societies, but every society has the problem of more or less satisfactory communication among them. The problem is actually a dilemma. On the one hand, each of the levels of the cultural hierarchy has essential functions, and therefore requires some support, maintenance, and approval. On the other hand, if there is to be a satisfactory degree of communication and solidarity in the society, there must be effective structures and processes for communication and fruitful interaction among the several levels of the cultural hierarchy. This dilemma is important, continuing, and confronts all societies.[26]

These structures and processes of cultural communication will vary in different types of society. In more hierarchical and authoritarian societies, cultural communication will more often be top-down, sparse, and probably poorly understood and somewhat resented by those at the lower levels of cultural achievement and possession. The Académie Française is a remnant of such a top-down structure. But in more democratic societies—indeed, this may be as much a requisite of democratic structures and processes as more explicitly political processes—cultural communication and interaction of all kinds, both upward (as the account of the history of jazz showed very well) and downwards, must be active, continuous, widespread, and recognized as

---

26. For a report on a recent panel discussion of this dilemma with regard to contemporary art criticism in the United States, see William Grimes, "Art Critics are Critical of Each Other's Criticism," *The New York Times*, May 18, 1996, 13, 17. The panel discussed conflicts among highbrow art critics and their different relations to middlebrow audiences.

essential. The National Endowments for the Arts and the Humanities were intended to be agencies for this kind of democratic cultural participation. Hence also the likelihood in the more democratic societies for there to be structures of universal and free education, as well as innumerable sources of latent and manifest cultural instruction and information about cultural novelties in public libraries, churches, newspapers, radio, TV,[27] now "cyberspace," and active local community cultural activities and participation. It is not just political associations and participation that are fundamental in a democracy. So also are cultural associations and participation essential to the "civil society" aspect of democracies. As all the criticism of the defects of the mass media in American society attest and probably exaggerate, these structures and processes of cultural communication in a democracy may be far from perfect;[28] they may be as hard to manage as well as the correlative political structures and processes, but they have their essential place in a satisfactory democracy.

Does "Class" Determine High and Low Status?

In popular thinking and also in some social science work there is an ideology that high status for cultural systems is determined by those in high class positions. This ideology, partly coming out of utilitarian premises, partly out of counter-establishment hostility, partly out of

---

27. The distinguished French sociologist Pierre Bourdieu, does not agree with this point about the importance of the mass media for democracy. His short, ninety-five-page polemic, *Sur la télévision* (Liber publishers), "denounced TV as a menace not only to highbrow culture but to democracy itself," according to a report in *Lingua Franca*, 7, no. 6 (1997), 22–3. This report says that Bourdieu's pamphlet has sold 100,000 copies and stirred up bitter debate. Bourdieu singled out for harsh criticism what he called the "fast thinkers," those who participate on TV talk shows. Is this another sign of the persisting elitism of French intellectual life?

28. For an illuminating discussion of the large cognitive and moral imperfections of American TV's daytime talk shows, which are a clear example of current lower culture, see Walter Goodman, "Daytime TV Talk: The Issue of Class," *The New York Times*, Nov. 1, 1995. Note that Mr Goodman, who is billed as a "cultural critic" for the *Times*, attributes these imperfections to "class" differences, not cultural ones.

general alienation with the society, is at least simplistic if not altogether wrong.[29] The relations between class and the high or low status of cultural systems are more complex than this ideology asserts it to be.

First of all, any such assertion should specify what it means by class. Does it mean power, or wealth, or "old family" status, or some combination of these? These different common definitions of class may play, as I have indicated above, for example in our discussion of patrons, some secondary role in establishing high or low status in some cultural systems, but the primary role everywhere is played by the educated experts who alone can bring to bear that generalized, systematic, and relatively comprehensive analysis and evaluation that truly defines some elements of a cultural system as high or low. Occasionally, of course, some wealthy or powerful person may have the knowledge and education and expert status that is essential in such definition. More often, it is likely that power, or wealth, or old family status come into play in supporting the final establishment of some elements of some cultural systems that experts have defined as high. They may serve as direct patrons of the producers of some types of cultural systems, of artists or composers, for example. Or they may serve as builders and maintainers of museums, concert halls, and theaters for the display and performance of high art. But it is not their primary function to be expert judges of that art. They may support and be guided by expert art dealers and musical and theater critics, but it is the expertise of these others that they are relying on.

For other cultural systems than art, music, theater, and dance, of course, even the supporting role of the powerful and wealthy may be less, and even then always indirect. Science, philosophy, scholarship, and theology are cultural systems where high and low are defined by knowledgeable and committed experts. It is the church, the university, and the foundation that are the primary supporters of the experts in these other cultural systems. The wealthy, powerful, and those of old family status have some influence on all of these, of course, but it is indirect, secondary, not primary. When we satisfactorily undertake scientific study of the problem of high and low status in the structure of

---

29. For agreement on this point, see Shrum, *Fringe and Fortune.* 29–33 and throughout.

various cultural systems, we abandon the simplistic ideology that it is class that is determinative. We study the complex ways that expertise, power, wealth, and education interact to maintain and advance change in the several cultural systems that make up the culture of a society as a whole.

Can We Trust the Cultural Experts?
The Problem of Relativism

We come, at last, to the key question about the structure of culture, how can we trust the experts, the cultural specialists, who make the final judgments about what is high, middle, or low in the contents of a cultural area? We have touched upon this matter in the discussions of class as a determinant of cultural standing and of the functions of the wealthy or powerful patrons of cultural activities. Here we need to confront it directly.

How can we know that the judgments of a community of experts in a cultural area are objective, based on some cumulative, internally self-critical, peer-controlled, endlessly correctable body of systematic, general, and comprehensive knowledge? The adherents of postmodernist and other kinds of philosophical relativism, who hold that all knowledge consists of biased readings of various "texts" or cultural ideas and symbols, do not accept the validity of judgments of established experts even when they say that their knowledge is cumulative, research-based in empirical fields like science, and peer-corrective. Such relativists are, of course, caught in what Jeffrey Alexander, in a general discussion of this problem, calls "the epistemological dilemma."[30] Radical relativism has no epistemological or social basis for its criticism of communities of cultural experts. It has no fixed philosophical or community of ex-

---

30. "Beyond the Epistemological Dilemma: General Theory in a Postpositivist Mode," *Sociological Forum*, 5 (1990), 531–44. For the particular field of science, see Stephen Cole, *Making Science: Between Nature and Society* (Cambridge, MA: Harvard University Press, 1992); and Paul Forman, "Truth and Objectivity. Part 1. Irony," *Science*, 269 (1995), 565–67, and Forman, "Truth and Objectivity. Part 2. Trust," *Science*, 260 (1995), 707–10. There is, of course, now a whole literature on postmodernism and other versions of "the epistemological dilemma" in other cultural areas.

pert standards for its critical discourse. The communities of cultural specialists, not the relativists, are our last, best hope for some objective understanding of their cultural areas. It is their judgments of high, middle, and low contents of those areas that we must and do trust.[31]

A Range, Not a Polarity:
The Importance of Middle-Level Culture

I need to suggest a caution. Both in the title of this chapter and in much, though not in all of its substance, I have, for reason of rhetorical convenience, spoken of the high-low aspect of the structure of cultural systems. That may be misleading. Both in the many actual references to middle levels of cultural structure and implicit in the oversimple high-low phrasing, I may have built up the impression that we are discussing a polarity and not a range of variation in the nature of cultural systems. But it is a range that exists, and that is what I want to emphasize here. There is a crude validity in the popular classification: highbrow, middlebrow, and lowbrow. In this chapter I have tried to transform that piece of middle-level sociology of culture into a more systematic, analytic sociological frame. Neither the analysis nor more popular statements like the "High-Low" show at the Museum of Modern Art and the literature on the subject that the curators of that show reviewed and criticized should neglect the importance of middle-level culture.

A polar concept of high and low ignores the massive amounts of middle-level culture in modern societies and its important functions.[32]

---

31. "Trust" here means two things: (1) expectations of competent performance; and (2) expectations of fiduciary responsibility to the society. For this analysis of trust, see Barber, *The Logic and Limits of Trust* (New Brunswick, NJ: Rutgers University Press, 1983).

32. On the nature and important functions of middle-brow culture, see two historical studies: Joan Shelley Rubin, *The Making of Middlebrow Culture* (Chapel Hill: University of North Carolina Press, 1992); and Janice Radway, *A Feeling For Books: The Book-of-the-Month Club, Literary Taste, and Middle-Class Desire* (Chapel Hill: University of North Carolina Press, 1997).

Radway's book has an excellent discussion of the conflicts among low, middle, and high levels of literary culture.

The creators and communicators of middle-level symbols, ideas, and their omnipresent artifactual embodiments in books and records are inevitable and necessary in modern society. So also are the newspapers and radio and TV stations. They are clearly necessary to communicate in middle-level cultural form such cultural systems as basic values and ideals, fundamental societal ideologies, science new and old, and religious ideas to the young. Indeed, since all of us are possessors at most of high culture in only one or a few areas, we all need middle-level intermediaries to instruct us in other areas at their middle level. Of course, for most people, middle- and low-level culture is all there is. Given the lack of a precise measuring instrument for the different levels of culture, the widespread use of the term "popular culture" is necessary as an imprecise reference to both middle- and low-level culture, although distinctions between these two levels are thereby blurred. Of course, because of a failure on both sides to understand the nature and functions of the different levels of culture, hostility and resentment occur, hostility that expresses itself in epithets from the higher level like "vulgarizers" and from the middle- and lower-levels of derisive terms like "double domes" and "dwellers in the ivory tower." To discuss the structure of cultural systems accurately, we need to distinguish a range of levels and not rest with the polarity of high and low.

5

❦ ❦ ❦

Cultural Tension and Conflict in the Academy: Scholars and Scientists Versus Ideologists and Reformers

We come, finally, to an aspect of culture and intellectual pursuits that uses and illustrates a good deal of the analysis contained in the earlier chapters, namely, the problem of intellectual tension and conflict in the academy: scholars and scientists versus ideologists and reformers. This is a problem that occurs elsewhere in modern society, but it is perhaps most clearly seen in the modern university.

A complete analysis of this problem would, of course, require attention to all the major variables of social system analysis—social structure, cultural structure, and personality structure. For brief example, as to social structural variables, matters of stratification (relative prestige of scientists vs. ideologists), matters of power between those who favor each of the two types of intellectual pursuit, and matters of different organizational and communication structures, all would require, and indeed have received, some close attention. In fact, too often these social structural variables, for example, power, have been overstressed, even absolutized. But here we focus on the importance of cultural structure, on the structured strain between two central types of intellectual pursuit, a strain that derives from differential commitment to two different components of the cultural system, science and ideology. Because of this limitation and special emphasis, it will be helpful to start with a brief recapitulation of some of the major points made in chapter 2, on culture and intellectual pursuits.

The cultural system of a society is made up of a considerable number of subsystems, each of which has some degree of autonomy but each of which is also interdependent with the others. Most of these subsystems—religion, art, philosophy, the sciences, for example—have become the subject in the university of their own special kind of intellectual pursuit by a community of cultural specialists. Ideology has no specialized university department but seems to occur to some extent in all of them.

Two of these cultural subsystems in focus here are science and ideology. The cultural system as a whole is no simple seamless web but rather a complex set of those subsystems, units that are often somewhat changing,[1] partly harmonious with or supportive of one another, partly conflicting or in competition with one another. Interdependency, in short, is not always positive, and vice versa; it may be positive, negative, or some mixture of the two. Thus, while there are ideologies that support science, there are some other ones that challenge it. And some science helps to make a strong case for an ideology; other science controverts it.

To understand just what the relations between any two subsystems of the cultural system are always requires careful study, preferably backed up by empirical research. In this chapter we look at the mixed interdependency, partly supportive, partly conflicting, of science and ideology. Unfortunately, not enough of the existing considerable attention paid to this problem is supported by research; there is more opinion than scientific analysis and careful research data in the discussions.

The Situation of the Modern University

While it is not the only place where the problem of the tension and conflict between science and objectivity, on the one side, and ideology

---

1. For a fascinating recent study of the changing religious beliefs and communal

and reformism, on the other, occurs in modern society—for example, it also occurs throughout journalism and the media generally—the modern university has become a central and important place for its occurrence. This is because the modern university has become the chief agency for the teaching, maintenance, and new creation of the established and ever-changing cultural tradition of the society. The modern university, in its complete form, in what is called the research university, or, in Clark Kerr's term, the "multiversity," pursues its teaching, maintenance, and creative functions with regard to all the subsystems of the culture, of what is accepted and valued as the cultural tradition.[2] The modern university is the home for the intellectual pursuits both of science and scholarship and of values and ideologies. The modern university supports cultural specialists not only in these two areas, of course, but in many others—music, art, philosophy, architecture, religion, literature, language—as well. In many of these fields, of course, the specialists are concerned not only for the technical subjects of the field but for the relevant values and ideologies. Philosophy is probably only the clearest case. The full diversity and complexity of the cultural tradition is present in the modern university.

It was not always thus. The intellectual pursuits that constitute the university have their origins, their proto-forms, as far back as Greek philosophy, mathematics, literature, medicine, and political and social science. These cultural substances were blended together in Greek thought in ways different from their specialized and differentiated forms that we take for granted today.[3] Still, even in these earliest forms,

ideologies of the Hindus and Muslims in post-Independence India, see Sudhir Kakar, *The Colors of Violence: Cultural Identities, Religion, and Conflict* (Chicago: University of Chicago Press, 1996).

2. There is, of course, a voluminous literature about the nature and problems of the modern university, just because of its central importance to the cultural tradition. For a recent exceptionally valuable set of essays by a group of distinguished university administrators and faculty, see Jonathan R. Cole, Elinor G. Barber, and Stephen R. Graubard, eds., *The Research University in a Time of Discontent* (Baltimore: Johns Hopkins University Press, 1994). This volume is an expansion of an earlier one presented as a volume of *Daedalus*, the journal of the American Academy of Arts and Sciences.

3. For an insightful account, avowedly only a sketch, of the development of culture and intellectual pursuits from Greek times to the present, see Talcott Parsons, " 'The Intellectuals,' A Social Role Category," in Philip Rieff, ed., *On Intellectuals* (New York: Anchor Books, 1970).

there exist what became eventually the specialized study of both values and ideologies and the study of science.

The earliest organizational forms of the university occur in medieval Europe, first in France and then in Britain. The chief, though not exclusive, focus of the cultural tradition in those early universities was religion and associated moral studies. Science had a relatively small place in the university until, beginning with the seventeenth-century Scientific Revolution,[4] it became the great competitor of religion, and eventually took over its predominant position in the nineteenth-century German university. In the twentieth century, and especially after World War II, the American universities became the premier world models. And, as the term "modern research university" connotes, it is science and other objective scholarship in all cultural fields that is now the university's hallmark. However, the study of values and commitment to associated ideologies remains important. It is these two essential parts of the modern university that present the complex interdependencies, positive and negative intermixed, that are the subject of this chapter.

Two Faces of the University

Actually, the modern university now has many faces: it not only is the teacher, custodian, and creator of the cultural tradition, but by some people it is now thought to have various other responsibilities: for example, among other things, for service to its local and national communities, for guarding the welfare of its students (though no longer strictly in loco parentis as it formerly was), and for cherishing the loyalty and seeking the support of its alumni. But here we are concentrating on only two of its concerns, for science and objective scholarship and for values and their associated ideologies. We need to understand each of these well to see what their complex interdependencies, especially their tension and conflict, are.

---

4. For a still essential but now only partial account of this Revolution, see Robert K. Merton, *Science, Technology, and Society in Seventeenth Century England* (Bruges, Belgium: OSIRIS, 1938).

Science and Objective Scholarship in the Modern University

Given its predominant position in the modern university, we begin with a discussion of science and objective scholarship before proceeding to a discussion of the importance for the university of values and ideologies. In his brilliant, lucid, and powerful account of what he calls the "Western Rationalistic Tradition," the philosopher John Searle both states its fundamental importance and specifies its components.[5] Here is his statement of its fundamental importance not only for the university and its science and objectivity but for the western cultural tradition as a whole.

> There is a conception of reality, and of the relationships between reality on the one hand and thought and language on the other, that has a long history in the Western intellectual tradition. Indeed, this conception is so fundamental that to some extent it defines that tradition. It involves a very particular conception of truth, reason, reality, rationality, logic, knowledge, evidence, and proof. Without too much of an exaggeration one can define this conception as "the Western Rationalistic Tradition." The Western Rationalistic Tradition takes different forms but it underlies the Western conception of science, for example.[6]

And here is his specification of the six essential features of the tradition "in its contemporary incarnation."[7] He states them in succinct form as tenets or propositions:

1. *"Reality exists independently of human representations."* (Italics in original.) "This view, called 'realism,' is the foundational principle of the Western Rationalist Tradition." This proposition is not

---

5. See his "Rationality and Realism, What Is At Stake?" in Cole, Barber, and Graubard, eds., *The Research University.*

6. Ibid., 57. Searle, as the committed scholar, is careful to point out that the Western Rationalistic Tradition has always been subject to challenge and it has evolved in response to those challenges. Moreover, he says, "another feature of the Western Rationalistic Tradition is its 'self-critical quality.' " "The idea of *critique* was always to subject any belief to the most rigorous standards of rationality, evidence, and truth" (58).

7. Ibid., 59. These features are stated and analyzed on pp. 60ff.

inconsistent with the view that there are large areas of reality that are indeed social constructs.

2. *"At least one of the functions of language is to communicate meanings from speakers to hearers and sometimes those meanings enable the communication to refer to objects and states of affairs in the world that exist independently of language.* . . . the philosophy of language became central to philosophy in general both because of its own intrinsic interest and because it was central to other problems in philosophy such as the nature of knowledge and truth."

3. *"Truth is a matter of the accuracy of representation."*

4. *"Knowledge is objective.* . . . knowledge does not depend on or derive from the subjective attitudes and feelings of particular investigators. . . . The point is that the objective truth or falsity of the claims made is totally independent of the motives, the morality, or even the gender, the race, or the ethnicity of the maker."[8]

5. *"Logic and rationality are formal.* . . . Logic and rationality provide standards of proof, validity, and reasonableness but the standards only operate on a previously given set of axioms, assumptions, goals, and objectives. Rationality as such makes no substantive claims."

6. *"Intellectual standards are not up for grabs. There are both objective and intersubjectively valid criteria of intellectual achievement and excellence."*

"All six of these principles are currently under attack in different forms," says Searle, an assertion we shall consider more fully later in this chapter in the discussion of what is called the "two cultures" problem. For the present, it is clear, though implicit, that he has a strong value commitment to this set of philosophical and methodological principles that he defines as essential to the Western Rationalistic Tradition as a whole and to the modern university and the science and objective scholarship that are supported there. We need now to look explicitly at the Western Cultural Tradition's values and their associ-

---

8. This is clearly a rebuttal of the relativist claims of many postmodern and constructivist theories of knowledge. Searle has a more detailed and direct critique of these theories at the end of his essay.

ated ideologies that support the six philosophical and methodological principles that constitute what Searle considers the "rationalistic" basis of that tradition.

The Values and Ideologies of the Modern University

In chapter 2 I defined values as the structures of moral preference that exist in all societies to guide actors in making decisions at certain inevitable action choice points, those points where alternative action possibilities exist. And I defined ideologies as those statements that justify or criticize the values and norms chosen by ourselves and others. Although the established, the main going values and ideologies are endlessly enunciated in high, middle, and low cultural forms, they are seldom codified in any final, authoritative way. We can point to many efforts at statements of a set of traditional cultural values, but at least in liberal societies, no simple official statements exist. The Declaration of Independence has a noble and eloquent statement of American values and their supporting ideologies,[9] the debates in Congress and judicial decisions all the way up to the Supreme Court declare values. Because religion and fundamental values are often closely connected they can be found in religious sermons, and of course they are omnipresent, as we saw in the small group discussion from Gamson's book, in everyday talk.

Lacking any simple, official statements then, I rely in this discussion on what I perceive to be a certain consensus on some values and ideologies that are considered essential in the western cultural tradition as a whole and for science and objective scholarship in the university specifically.[10] I concentrate here on two values: rationality and universal-

---

9. See Pauline Maier, *American Scripture: Making the Declaration of Independence* (New York: Knopf, 1997). The term "scripture" was, of course, deliberately chosen by Maier to signify the moral/ideological character of the Declaration.

10. For a much earlier, still valid, I think, extensive account of western cultural values, see Bernard Barber, *Science and the Social Order* (Glencoe, IL: The Free Press, 1952), Ch. I, The Nature of Science: The Place of Rationality in Human Society; Ch. II, The Historical Development of Science: Social Influences on the Development of Science; and, Ch. III, Science in Modern Society: Its Place in Liberal and Authoritarian Society.

ism (or equality). While these two values are basically supportive of science and objective scholarship in the university, they also, ironically, have some negative effects in the form of ideologies that challenge what Searle calls the Western Rationalistic Tradition. We shall consider both sides of this intermixture of effects; for now, the positive effects, and in due course, through a variety of historical and current materials, some of the negative ones.

Rationality[11]

Rational empirical behavior and thought occurs to some extent in all societies, even the simplest. Human life is impossible without it, both with regard to how we deal with the natural world and how we treat our families and fellows. By the value of rationality we mean something more than behavior. We mean the morally approved, the emotionally supported, the "institutionalized," as the sociologist would say, preference for rational practice throughout wide areas of the society. The value of rationality results in the critical approach to all the phenomena of human existence in the attempt to reduce them to ever more consistent, orderly, and generalized forms of understanding.

Rationality as a value is specifically different from its opposite, the value of traditionalism, which has been the predominant value in all types of non-modern society and, of course, still persists to some extent even in modern society. Traditionalism values whatever exists, on its own terms, simply because it has always existed and has been morally approved by the ancestors. In such a value regime, there is no support for social or cultural criticism in terms of rational consistency and generalization. The "rational bent" of modern man, which Thorstein Veblen was one of the first to compare with the values and habits of people in other societies, leads modern people to question the world in every direction, to analyze all that has been passed down merely by "the rule of custom." The modern world values and justifies the role of reason, it devalues and criticizes the rule of custom and ritual.

The value of rationality, so important for science and objective

---

11. I am here following the discussion at p. 62.

scholarship, prevails throughout modern society. Everybody, we feel, has the right to ask questions and satisfy him- or herself. Rationality is not just a right, it is a duty; as a result, rationality is an active force in modern society. No realm of the natural or social worlds is immune to penetration by the active rationality prescribed by our cultural approval of this value. Inevitably, active rationality arouses resistance in some of the areas it seeks to investigate or reform, but overall it persists as one of our central values.

We might note here the strong connection of the value of rationality with important western religious beliefs. For this analysis we owe a fundamental debt to the scholarship of the great German sociologist, Max Weber, and to his comparative sociology of religion on the "great religions" of the world (Hinduism, Confucianism, Christianity, Judaism, Islam), a sociology he created on the basis of his remarkable scholarship.[12]

On the basis of his study of the different world religions, Weber concluded that the Graeco-Judaic-Christian religious beliefs were more favorable than other kinds of religious belief to both the value of rationality and to the practice of everyday rationality. Among these important religious beliefs were that the supernatural and natural worlds were separate, that God was rational and that the natural world reflected that rationality; moreover that "man" could discover God's rationality in the world and act upon it. These beliefs, so important for science and objective scholarship and the modern university were not present in the other great world religions. They had what Weber called a more "magical image" of the world.

Especially important for the modern world, Weber thought, was Calvinist Protestantism, which brought the great forces of medieval Catholic rationalism into everyday life. Calvinist theology held that it was everyone's religious duty to order his or her "this-worldly" activities of all kinds in the most rational fashion possible. Gradually, of

---

12. The best known of Weber's monographs is, of course, *The Protestant Ethic*, but see also *The Religion of India*, *Ancient Judaism*, *The Religion of China*, and *The Sociology of Religion*, all published by the Free Press. For what is still an excellent account of Weber on religion, see Talcott Parsons, *The Structure of Social Action* (New York: American Book Company, 1937). There is now a whole "Weber industry" of scholarship especially in Germany but also in the United States.

course, this religious belief has been secularized but still holds sway in science, economic activities, and behavior most generally.

Universalism/Equality

The other central value in the western cultural tradition, universalism/equality, also has an origin in religious beliefs. If we feel we should apply universalistic/egalitarian values to everyone, it is because we are acting on the secularized version of the Judaeo-Christian belief in the brotherhood of man in God, the belief that we are all God's children. We now speak of "the brotherhood of man," *tout court*, but it carries the same moral weight as its religious antecedent.[13]

The value of universalism/equality requires that every person should have the opportunity to pursue his calling in the world and should have his or her performance judged on the same standards, regardless of particularistic values such as kinship, ethnicity, or race. Such a value is obviously of the greatest importance for all social activities based on talents and so applies everywhere in the world of work and other social activities. It is of essential importance to the proper functioning of science and objective scholarship in the modern university.

Some Examples of Cultural Conflict in the University and Elsewhere in Modern Society

We turn now to some examples, some illustrations in the form of various past and present discussions and events, of the cultural conflict I have outlined up to this point. Ignoring some even earlier occasions, we concentrate on discussions and events that go back about forty years and continue right into the immediate present. Each discussion and event seems radically new to many of those who get involved in it, but the basic cultural conflict is always there. There seems to be no sign

---

13. In speaking of other blacks as "brothers," thus excluding whites, blacks have retreated from the value of universalism to an ethnic or racial particularism. The same kind of retreat is implicit, on the gender side, when feminists speak of other women as "sisters." Both these terms violate the value of universalism, of the unity of all people regardless of gender, race, ethnicity, or whatever.

that this conflict will end any time soon. We start with C. P. Snow's discussion of what he called "the two cultures."

The Two Cultures, Redux

In 1959 there appeared a very small book, just a small pamphlet, only fifty-two pages long, that was destined to have a very large effect on the discussion by the educated classes in Great Britain and the United States of the conflict between science and other values and ideologies. That book was *The Two Cultures and The Scientific Revolution*, by C. P. Snow (later Lord Snow).[14] The book, and Snow's discussion and term, "the two cultures," have become a standard and a reference point for subsequent writings on this problem right up to the present.[15]

Snow's book is the published version of the honorific Rede Lecture that he delivered before a prestigious audience at Cambridge University. Before such an audience, which prided itself on its scientific and general scholarly distinction, Snow properly felt he had to legitimate his authority to discuss the large topic he set for his lecture. Snow tells the audience and his readers that he was the scion of generations of workingmen and laborers who, nevertheless, had managed to win for himself a place at Cambridge in the 1930s. Snow studied physics and mathematics at a time when Cambridge gloried in such professors as the great physicist Rutherford and the outstanding mathematician, G. H. Hardy.[16] Snow had a personal acquaintance with both. With Hardy, it was a long and intimate friendship.

---

14. Cambridge, England: Cambridge University Press, 1959. An earlier, briefer version, Snow tells us in a footnote, was published as "The 'Two Cultures,'" in *New Statesman*, October 6, 1956. Indeed, Snow further tells us that he had been thinking about this problem much earlier on, "long before I put it on paper."

15. For example, it is referred to in the next book we shall discuss, one that recently also aroused a storm of controversy, Paul R. Gross and Norman Levitt, *Higher Superstition: The Academic Left and Its Quarrels with Science* (Baltimore: Johns Hopkins Press, 1994), 7, 244.

16. On Rutherford, who was one of the giants of the field, see any history of modern physics. On Hardy, see his charming autobiography. *A Mathematician's Apology* (Cambridge, England: Cambridge University Press, 1940), reprinted 1967 with a fifty-eight-page foreword by none other than C. P. Snow. In his Preface to the original printing, Hardy acknowledges "Dr. C. P. Snow" as a reader of that printing who made "valuable criticisms."

After a brief period in the 1930s as a working scientist, Snow was caught up in World War II as a scientific administrator and adviser. After the war he became a full-time member of the Scientific Branch of the Civil Service. At the time of his Lecture, he had already spent thirty years there. He reports that, among other activities in this position, he interviewed thousands of working scientists. The interviews were a powerful lesson on the matter of the literary ignorance of these scientists.

During the period, Snow's vocation for substantive science turned into a literary vocation and he became a prolific and successful novelist. He wrote a series of well-received books about the lives and problems, both scientific and human, of working scientists and university professors. As a part of his new vocational commitment as a writer, he came to associate with other writers and also became an active participant in British literary circles. Snow was, for a good while, living two different lives, one with scientists and the other with literary types, and so felt he had a singular knowledge of their two different and opposing cultures, their different values and ideologies. He had intimate friends in both circles.[17]

Most of all, as a result of his unusual experience, Snow says in his book, he was struck and dismayed by the complete ignorance that both of these two groups had of each other's culture. Although he had greatest familiarity, obviously, with his British colleagues, he says that his lesser experience in the United States still brought him to the same conclusion about this mutual ignorance. Indeed, he goes so far as to say it prevails "throughout the West." Is this an ignorance that prevails to a great extent right up to the present? As to Britain, Snow attributes it primarily to the great early and continuing specialization of the educational system. He felt there was somewhat less of this in the United States, but still a great deal. Mutual ignorance, Snow felt, also was

---

17. Incidentally, in his book Snow reports an anecdote that may shed some light on the origin of the common use of the term "intellectuals." He says that the literary intellectuals, "who incidentally, while no one was looking, took to referring to themselves as 'intellectuals' as though there were no others. I remember G. H. Hardy once remarking to me in mild puzzlement, some time in the 1930s: 'Have you noticed how the word "intellectual" is used nowadays? There seems to be a new definition which certainly doesn't include Rutherford or Eddington or Dirac or Adrian or me. It does seem rather odd, don't y'know.' "

accompanied, "sometimes (particularly among the young)" by "hostility and dislike." The two groups have a "distorted image" of one another.

Non-scientists, Snow felt, thought of scientists as "brash and boastful," "shallowly optimistic, unaware of man's condition." Of course, these negative judgments imply the non-scientist's own values and ideology: they themselves are modest, properly pessimistic, and aware of the tragic elements in man's condition. And the scientists express their own values and ideology by judging the non-scientist to be "totally lacking in foresight, peculiarly unconcerned with their brother men, in a deep sense anti-intellectual, anxious to restrict art and thought to the existential moment." It is not quite clear what Snow meant here, but about some matters he was as clear as clear can be. He felt the scientists were certainly optimistic. As he put it in his famous phrase, "they have the future in their bones." Even where the scientist is aware of the possibility of tragedy in the condition of particular individuals, there is no reason why this has to be true of the social condition as a whole. Scientists tend to be "unbelievers," Snow thought, literary people the opposite. Snow had the insight that I asserted as a general point in the chapter on ideology, that each set of values and ideologies breeds its opposite: He said, "the feeling of one pole becomes the anti-feelings of the other." The unscientific culture is often "on the point of turning anti-scientific." Of course we should add, "and vice versa."

It was Snow's view (his ideology, as primarily a scientist?) that it was the traditional unscientific culture "which manages the western world." Snow felt that the polarization of values and ideologies between scientists and self-styled intellectuals was "a sheer loss to us all." And here is where Snow's own value-preference appears most clearly. He was disturbed not by the effects of this polarization on the university, although they occurred there too,[18] but by their effects on the condition of the world at large. He was especially disturbed by the continued existence of a split between the rich industrial countries and the poor non-industrial ones. He thought that the only way to remove this difference, this injustice, was for the rich countries to use their scientific culture to make the poor countries a little more equal to

---

18. See his classic novel of politics in the university, *The Masters*.

them, to help them to become industrial themselves. It was a noble ideal, but the world has gone in that direction only a little way, not all the way as Snow hoped. This continued inequality is not, of course, the product solely of the existence of the two cultures; it has many sources, but the lack of understanding and cooperation between the two cultures has certainly not helped to bring about Snow's desired social change.[19]

The Evolution of the Two Cultures Conflict: Gross and Levitt's Plaint and Complaint

In the nearly forty years since the publication of Snow's *The Two Cultures*, the western university has flourished mightily and become ever more complex, ever more inclusive of the whole range of intellectual pursuits that our culture requires and creates. So also has the conflict between the two cultures become more complex, the conflict between science and objective scholarship on the one hand, and values and associated ideologies on the other. Nowhere, perhaps, has this conflict been more fully displayed recently than in the book, *Higher Superstition: The Academic Left and Its Quarrels with Science* by two distinguished natural scientists, Professors Paul R. Gross (a biologist) and Norman Levitt (a mathematician).[20] Their book is a much more complex ideological justification[21] for science than Snow's Rede Lecture was and a much more detailed account of what they consider the several erring constituents of the "other" culture than Snow's was of "the literary intellectuals."

The basic plaint of Gross and Levitt is that science, the great achievement of western culture, is no longer held in the respect and admiration it should have. Their basic complaint is against those they feel are responsible in some essential way for this rejection of science,

---

19. Snow was idealistic but not soft-headed. In the conclusion of his book he says, "On the other hand, I confess, and I should be less than honest if I didn't, that I can't see the political techniques through which the good human capabilities of the West can get into action."

20. Baltimore: Johns Hopkins Press, 1994.

21. See especially Ch. Two, "Some History and Politics: Natural Science and Its Natural Enemies."

scholars engaged in four different kinds of intellectual pursuit whom they vaguely describe as "the academic left" and who cultivate such intellectual pursuits as (1) "social constructivism" both in general and particularly in the sociology of science; (2) feminism; (3) postmodernism, which often has a radically relativist ontology; and (4) some extreme versions of environmentalism that romanticize nature and blame science for what they consider all the world's environmental troubles.

Gross and Levitt have written an eloquent, powerful, very well informed, not always consistent or sound book that is basically an expression of their own western values and an attack on those who they think do not share them. The very title of their book, *Higher Superstition*, is an accusation of irrationality against those they criticize and an implicit claim, contrariwise, to the fundamental rationality of science. Although they lump these irrationalists, these opponents of science, together in the title and throughout the text as "the academic left," and although they several times try to justify their use of this term, they do not succeed. It is clear certainly that the academic left are not necessarily on the political left although many of them seem to them to lean that way; indeed, many scientists are of that persuasion. Gross and Levitt's academic left are by no means an organized group or even a loose coalition; some of them are indifferent to or even hostile to one another. They seem to exist only as a set of different kinds of intellectual pursuits opposed to science, "unambiguously hostile," and, Gross and Levitt admit at one point, which they find it "convenient" to lump together as "the academic left."[22]

We should emphasize that, for Gross and Levitt, the prime Western value is rationality, not equality; they seldom mention equality in their plaint and complaints. For at least one of their target groups, however, namely the feminists, equality is perhaps the prime value. But neither the feminists nor Gross and Levitt's other target groups accept the

---

22. Sometimes they speak of their academic left as a "community," sometimes as "an interlinked set of communities," sometimes just as a "large and influential segment of the American academic community." They are sufficiently aware of the vagueness of this term that they say, early on, that they use it "for convenience but with great misgiving." At one point, Gross and Levitt say that they considered but then rejected the term "perspectivist left" instead of "academic left." The former would have emphasized the common philosophical element in their target groups.

charge of irrationality. Indeed, they all feel they are themselves fully rational, though not necessarily in the same way as the established scientists. They are just going beyond the philosophical, methodological, and substantive shortcomings of current science and its conceptions of rationality. After looking at Gross and Levitt's detailed complaints against each of their targets (they devote a detailed chapter to each one), we shall report the responses and values that each of these several target groups present. The "two cultures" conflict has, as I have said, some social-structural sources also, but the cultural conflict seems to be primary. It is a conflict that is partly due to differential emphasis on different values and partly to differences of view about what agreed-upon values specifically entail. Thus, in general, cultural conflict may occur not only between radically different cultures, as one limited conception of such conflict has it, but also between quite similar cultures and, of course, people in the same culture.

Values and associated ideologies underlie all social activities, including science and objective scholarship. Gross and Levitt's distress is clearly basically cultural, a matter of basic values and ideologies, not a matter of practical interests. This can be seen in the fact that they do not feel that working scientists need to be "unduly alarmed" that scientific practice will be affected in the short run. At least that is true for natural science, if not for objective scholarship in social science, history, and the humanities. It is the longer run, and the changes in the essential character of the larger western society, they say, that they are worried about. (They are not worried for the less-developed world, as Snow was.) The diverse but cumulating attacks on science and rationality, they feel, will ultimately be destructive not just of science but of the basic cultural character, the basic values, of western society.

To back up their general complaints, Gross and Levitt see it as their rational scholarly obligation to cite chapter and verse about the antiscientific views of the four kinds of intellectual pursuits they have singled out for criticism.

Edinburgh Sociology of Science

Gross and Levitt start with a group of very able and productive philosophers and sociologists of science that has emerged and won great attention and admiration during the last twenty-five years. The philosophers David Bloor and Barry Barnes and the sociologists Harry Collins, Steven Woolgar, Michael Mulkay, and co-authors Stephen Shapin and Simon Schaffer are some of the central British figures in this group. Important similar sociologists of science are Karen Knorr-Cetina in Germany, Bruno Latour in France, and Arie Rip and Wiebe Bijker in Holland. In addition to their several books, the work of all these and many similar sociologists of science, together with reviews of their work, can be found in the journal *Social Studies of Science*, ably and devotedly edited at the University of Edinburgh's Science Studies Unit by David Edge, a radio astronomer who has himself contributed substantively to this school's work.[23]

Gross and Levitt start with the sociology of science for a number of good reasons.[24] First, the work is explicitly and almost wholly about natural science. Second, they see the errors about science of this work as particularly stark. And, third, they feel that their other targets, such as postmodernism and feminism, have been perversely influenced by the sociology of science.

Gross and Levitt say immediately that they concede that there is much good sociology of science; they give some examples both of the aspects of science that are indeed influenced by social structural and cultural factors and where there already exists some solid empirical research on these topics. They call this to-them-acceptable kind of sociology of science the "weak program" to distinguish it from the abhorrent strong program created and so-labelled by the Edinburgh group. The strong program, they say, in contrast to what they concede is the validity of the weak program, is the creation of "perverse theo-

---

23. For a useful critical guide to this literature and to its bibliography, see Warren Schmaus, Ullica Segerstrale, and Douglas Jesseph, "A Manifesto on the 'Hard Program' in the Sociology of Scientific Knowledge," *Social Epistemology*, 6 (1992), 243–65. What Schmaus and his colleagues call the "hard program" was named the "strong program" originally by Bloor, and that term is used by Gross and Levitt.

For a statement on the "strong program" by myself, see the brief paper, "Acceptance," in *Science, Technology, and Human Values*, 21 (1996), 342–346. This paper contains the remarks made on the occasion of the award of the Bernal Prize by the Society for the Social Studies of Science of which this journal is the official publication. The paper is both admiring and critical, admiring of its empirical work, critical of its ontological relativism and its leftist "interest" sociology.

24. See chapter 3, "The Cultural Construction of Cultural Constructivism."

ries" and is, as they say in one of their frequent unguarded emotional moments, "unalloyed twaddle." As ideologists for science, Gross and Levitt, feeling very strongly about their central values, manifest the emotionality that is common in such ideological situations.

According to Gross and Levitt, the "perverse theory" is, in essence, the philosophical position that science is totally "socially constructed," so that there is no "real nature" out there. Science, further, is only the constructions of an arrogant and powerful group claiming to have an exclusive "scientific" monopoly on knowledge of natural reality.[25] In its extreme version, the theory holds that western science is just another view of the world, on a par with mysticism, superstition, quackery, and other cultist theories.

Here is Gross and Levitt's verbatim summary of what they call the perverse theory:

> Science is a highly elaborated set of conventions brought forth by one particular culture (our own) in the circumstances of one particular historical period; thus it is not, as the standard view would have it, a body of knowledge and testable conjecture concerning the real world. It is a discourse, devised by and for one "interpretive community," under terms created by the complex net of social circumstance, political opinion, economic incentive, and ideological climate that constitutes the ineluctable human environment of the scientist. Thus, orthodox science is but one discursive community among the many that now exist and that have existed historically. Consequently its truth claims are irreducibly self-referential in that they can be upheld only by the standards that define "the scientific community" and distinguish it from other social formations.
>
> It must follow, then, that science deludes itself when it asserts a particular privileged position in respect to its ability to "know" reality. . . . Even—now especially—the practices that most particularly embody the sacred "objectivity" of science—experiment and observation—are inescapably *textual* practices meaningless outside the community that endows them with meaning.

This point of view, say Gross and Levitt, obviously "leaves no ground whatsoever for distinguishing reliable knowledge from super-

---

25. This position of ontological relativism is, of course, strongly criticized by many philosophers on philosophical grounds. For the best critique by a sociologist of science, see Stephen Cole, *Making Science: Between Nature and Reality* (Cambridge, MA: Harvard University Press, 1992).

stition." Further, it implies that "social and political interests dictate scientific 'answers.' " Science becomes merely a parable, an allegory, a mythic structure.

Given this view, it is no wonder that Gross and Levitt consider the strong program the height of irrationality and a danger to science and the larger Western value of rationality that creates and supports it. This is not, of course, a conclusion that the Edinburgh sociologists of science accept. They think of their theory and position as the latest advance in "certified knowledge," which Robert Merton has defined as one of the essential elements of genuine scientific knowledge. They do not grant the argument made by many of their critics that their radical relativism subverts their own position. Some of them, to be sure, back off from the extreme form of the strong program. Harry Collins, for example, who has done several extremely interesting empirical studies of both mainline and marginal science has said that he finds the extreme position just a useful "heuristic device" for leading him into empirical investigations of the social aspects of science. For now, what is anathema to Gross and Levitt remains a strong philosophical and methodological set of received assumptions in the practice of a quite large community of sociologists of science who are inspired by the strong program.[26]

Postmodernism in American Humanities and Social Science Departments

Gross and Levitt's second target is the postmodern thought that in the last twenty-five years has "inflected the thinking," they say, "of hosts of scholars . . . chiefly in departments of English, comparative literature, art history, and the like; but anyone familiar with contemporary American universities is well aware of how far it has spread into

---

26. For a very recent rejection of the critique by Gross and Levitt (and others) of the Edinburgh School's alleged epistemological relativism and alleged denial of the existence of a "natural reality," see a lengthy, detailed, heavily documented editorial by David Edge, *Social Studies of Science*, 26 (1996), 723–732. Edge says that a recent textbook by Barry Barnes, David Bloor, and John Henry (central figures in the Strong Program school), *Scientific Knowledge: A Sociological Analysis* (Chicago: University of Chicago Press, 1996), supports the clarificatory defense presented in his editorial.

such unlikely areas as sociology, history, political science, anthropology, and philosophy." Their complaint against postmodernism is that it is irrational, radically relativistic, and even ultimately "nihilistic." It destroys the possibility of reliable knowledge not only in science but in all the intellectual pursuits where objective cultural scholarship exists.[27] Specifically as to science, that is seen by postmodernism as "simply a cultural construct which, in both form and content . . . is deeply inscribed with assumptions about domination, mastery, and authority."

As to what postmodernism specifically is, Gross and Levitt say they feel they have to discuss it seriously, even though they consider it "too variegated and shifty to allow easy categorization, and too willfully intent on avoiding definitional precision. There is even a risk of misleading in calling it a body of ideas, for postmodernism is more a matter of attitude and emotional tonality than of rigorous axiomatics."

Gross and Levitt charge that postmodernism is basically a "negation—a negation of themes that have reigned in liberal intellectual life of the West since the Enlightenment." Postmodernism defines itself as an "antithetical doctrine" to the central intellectual project of the Enlightenment, which is to build up "a sound body of knowledge about the world the human race confronts." The Enlightenment "project" is considered by postmodernism to be "futile, self-deceptive, and worst of all, *oppressive*." "Representations" and "reality" are considered to be inherently antagonistic, and this assumption justifies both the postmodernist confident disregard for established facts and for their arbitrary readings of the meaning of "texts." "Reality" is "chimerical" and all "human awareness is a creature and a prisoner of the language games that encode it."

Postmodernism, further, rejects the Enlightenment goal of universal knowledge. It holds that all knowledge is "local," or "situated," the product of a social class limited by its prejudices, interests, and historical conditions. "There is no knowledge, then," say Gross and Levitt, "there are merely stories, narratives, devised to satisfy the human need to make sense of the world." Irrational indeed, Gross and Levitt are

---

27. See chapter 4, "The Realm of Idle Phrases: Postmodernism, Literary Theory, and Cultural Criticism." This chapter title expresses the gist of Gross and Levitt's critique.

saying. And this irrational postmodernism infects the "highly politicized" area of women's studies and also the whole new field of "cultural studies,"[28] which is now "the institutional embodiment of postmodernism."

Gross and Levitt, strongly committed as they are to the Enlightenment value and ideology for rationality, are also, as often happens with ideologists, strongly opposed to what they consider their opposite, the ideologies of postmodernism. Here is their example of these ideologies: "*Resistance, subversion, and transgression* are among the most popular postmodernist nouns and the sense in which they are used clearly conveys the idea that bourgeois society, founded on racism, sexism, and the enforcement of rigid social roles, is under attack, its vulnerabilities being exposed."

Once again, we see how the two cultures, the one of science and objective scholarship, but holding strong supporting values and ideologies, and the other, heavily based on different values and supporting ideologies, though claiming to be as rational as established natural science, perhaps more so, exist in a present state of conflict.

Feminism and Science

Since their critique of feminist science overlaps with what we have just examined for the sociology of science and postmodernism, we can be brief in the discussion of Gross and Levitt's treatment of feminism and science.[29] Gross and Levitt begin by conceding two important

---

28. For more on the field of "cultural studies," see the earlier account in chapter 2 of this book.

29. See Chapter Five, "Auspicating Gender," Neither in the text nor in footnotes do the authors explain their selection of the little-used term "auspicating" nor does an unabridged dictionary shed any light on the matter.

Although discussion of the contents of this chapter is brief, the chapter itself is long. It contains detailed discussions of several feminist analyses of substantive scientific matters, such as algebra (presumably by Levitt, the mathematician) and various biological topics (presumably by Gross, the biologist). These detailed discussions, of course, point out the errors in substantive feminist science.

We should also note that we will not take up Gross and Levitt's fourth target, environmentalism. Enough is enough. See the discussion of environmentalism as an ideology in Chapter Three.

points. First, they acknowledge the long-time discrimination against women among scientists, both in barring them from entry and treating them badly if they did gain entry. They feel that such discrimination is now diminished and perhaps disappearing. Second, they acknowledge that many recent studies of women's past contributions to science have been valid and valuable contributions to the history of science. On both scores, women are now getting the justice they deserve. Gross and Levitt might more clearly have pointed also to the value of the new attention by women scientists to problems peculiarly important to women, such as in reproductive biology.

Despite these two acknowledgments, however, they strongly reject, of course, a widespread and influential strain of feminist science that criticizes the basic epistemology and methodology of science. Lately, they say, "a new academic industry has sprung up: feminist criticism of science." Further, this new criticism "claims to go to the heart of the methodological, conceptual, and epistemological foundations of science. It claims to provide the basis for a reformulation of science that reaches deeply into its content, its ideas, and its findings. The key process of this critique is insistence that inasmuch as science has until now been a male enterprise, it is ipso facto biased by assumptions derived from the patriarchal values of Western society."

Gross and Levitt emphasize the influence of postmodern thinking on feminist science. They allege that "many feminist tracts accept and defend the notion that there is no 'objective' science, merely a variety of 'perspectives,' one of which—patriarchal science—has been 'valorized' and 'empowered' so as to preclude until now the possibility of feminist science." The original goal of feminist science, to eliminate discrimination, has now been transformed into the "more ambitious project to refashion the epistemology of science from the roots up."

Gross and Levitt see this, of course, as another attack on the essential Western value of rationality. They do not see that it may be an extreme result of the feminist demand for the realization of that other essential Western value, equality.

Beyond Gross and Levitt: The Sokal "Hoax"

Although Gross and Levitt could not conceal their contempt and anger for postmodernism and associated doctrines in the Edinburgh school's sociology of science and in radical feminism, and although they sometimes spoke of these targets of their criticism as ludicrous and ridiculous, as "the realm of idle phrases," still usually they tried hard to stay in the serious and discursive mode appropriate to an essay in objective critical scholarship. Going beyond Gross and Levitt, however, Professor Alan D. Sokal, a physicist at New York University, attacked these same targets with a powerful exercise in parody and in what members of the target groups, charging deception, called by the more invidious term, "hoax."

The parody consisted of an esoterically nonsensical article, presumably based on physics, by Sokal seeking to ridicule postmodernist studies of natural science. The piece was submitted to and accepted by the distinguished editors, based in the humanities, of the prestigious postmodernist journal, *Social Text*, for an issue with the theme of the "Science Wars," an issue which was planned as a critique of the Gross and Levitt book.[30] Sokal then himself exposed what he had done in *Lingua Franca: The Review of Academic Life*, a freelance journal priding itself on revealing the contentious and seamy side of American academic life.[31] In another, later article, addressed to the editors of *Social Text*, but which they refused to publish, Sokal sought to explain the political reasons for his parody. He has been, he said, and continues to be a political leftist and is dismayed by the harmful effects that the foolish leftism of the postmodernists have on desirable leftist political and social programs. (Same values, he says, but cognitive differences lead to cultural conflict.) He wishes, he says, to "make a small contribution to a dialogue on the left between humanists and natural scientists—'two cultures' that contrary to some optimistic pronouncements

30. Sokal, "Transgressing the Boundaries—Toward A Transformative Hermeneutics of Quantum Gravity," *Social Text*, Spring/Summer, 1996, 217–252. *Social Text* is published by the Duke University Press, of which Prof. Stanley Fish is executive editor. Fish is one of the great powers in English studies and cultural studies more generally. He responded to the Sokal article in a piece on the op ed page of the *New York Times*, which shall be mentioned again below.

31. Sokal, "A Physicist Experiments With Cultural Studies," *Lingua Franca* 6 (May/June) 1996, 62–64. Sokal says that his parodic adventure was inspired by the Gross and Levitt book. Note that in this title Sokal has broadened out his target from postmodernism to "cultural studies." On cultural studies, see Chapter Two of this book.

(mostly by the former group) are probably farther apart in mentality than at any time in the past fifty years." This second article was finally published by the long-time leftist journal, *Dissent*.[32]

Although seeking to explain his political purpose in the "Afterword" article, Sokal takes nothing back from his original critique of postmodernism. "Like the genre it is meant to satirize," says Sokal,

> myriad examples of which can be found in any reference list, my article is a melange of truths, half-truths, quarter-truths, falsehoods, non sequiturs, and syntactically correct sentences that have no meaning whatsoever. . . . I also employed some other strategies that are well established (albeit sometimes inadvertently) in the genre: appeals to authority in lieu of logic, speculative theories passed off as established science, strained and even absurd analogies, rhetoric that sounds good but whose meaning is ambiguous, and confusion between the technical and the everyday senses of English words.

In response to Sokal's parody and his *Lingua Franca* article, as might only have been expected against the background of the current cultural conflict between the "two cultures," a storm of controversy has arisen, with contributions from leading representatives of science and equally prominent representatives of the humanities. This storm has manifested itself not only in such high culture journals as the *New York Review of Books*, but also on the op-ed pages of the *New York Times*, thus getting a much wider audience. Our society now has not only a much larger population than it used to have of scientists and scholars following specialized intellectual pursuits but also a similarly larger population of those who take an interest in the affairs of universities and of science and scholarship. Recognizing this, the various media now regularly follow these affairs, especially those that involve conflict. The *New York Times* has become an important journal, at high and middle cultural levels, of news and ideologies about both the substance and the problems of science, not only every day but especially in its special Science edition on Tuesdays.

On the side of science and Sokal, Professor Steven Weinberg, for-

---

32. "Transgressing the Boundaries: An Afterword," *Dissent*, Fall, 1996, 93–99. Sokal is an excellent writer. Much of what he says in this article overlaps with Gross and Levitt's critique.

merly of Harvard and more recently of the University of Texas, a Nobel Prize laureate in particle physics, weighed in with a long article in the *New York Times Review of Books* approving of Sokal's parody, which he called a "prank" he found amusing.[33] Weinberg, who has recently published a large book, *Dreams of a Final Theory: The Search for the Fundamental Laws of Nature* for a general audience, prides himself on his knowledge of and concerns for the larger issues of the nature of science. Most of his article was an extended critique of the postmodernists' ignorance of both the substance and essential nature of science, and an exposition of the nature of science very much overlapping with the views expressed in his book. In sum, he says, although Sokal was not the first to address these issues,

> he has done a great service in raising them so dramatically. They are not entirely academic issues, in any sense of the word academic. If we think that scientific laws are flexible enough to be affected by the social setting of their discovery, then some may be tempted to press scientists to discover laws that are more proletarian or feminine or American or religious or Aryan or whatever else it is they want. This is a dangerous path and more is at stake than just the health of science. . . . We will need to confirm and strengthen the vision of a rationally understandable world if we are to protect ourselves from the irrational tendencies that still beset humanity.

Once again, as with Gross and Levitt, we see that rationality is king for the scientist.

On the side of postmodernism, at least as represented by *Social Text*, both Professor Stanley Fish and Professor Steve Fuller, in their contributions to the *New York Times*, angrily complained that Sokal had abused the trust of the editors of *Social Text* in his credentials as a physicist.[34] As for the editors of *Social Text* themselves, they excused themselves for publishing Sokal's article by saying they were just "a journal of opinion" and did not evaluate articles. Unfortunately, so much the worse for their credibility!

---

33. "Sokal's Hoax," XLIII (1996), pp. 11–15.

34. Steve Fuller, letter to the editor, the *New York Times*, May 23, 1996, 28; and Fish, op ed article, "Professor Sokal's Bad Joke," ibid., May 21, 1996, 23. Fuller is an Edinburgh school sociologist of science.

As to Weinberg's defense of Sokal and science, a series of letters by various Yale, Princeton, and Rutgers professors in history and the humanities accepts his critique of *Social Text*, but are otherwise interesting as sensible critics of Weinberg's article and of scientists in general.[35] First, there is a charge against Weinberg of "dualism" and seeming "reduction" of all truth to science, perhaps particularly to Weinberg's own specialty, particle physics. The complaint is that Weinberg separates science too much from the rest of culture. It is correct that in Weinberg's article there is no clear acknowledgment, as there was in Gross and Levitt, of the value of the weak program in the sociology of science. And second, there is a complaint about Weinberg's "assumption of overwhelming authority for science." Some of the authors of these letters are historians of science anxious to reject what they see as the polarization between *Social Text's* postmodernism and Weinberg's absolutism on the "truth" of science. In his response, Weinberg rejects the charge of dualism and acknowledges his acceptance of some social and cultural influences on science.

There is the beginning here of a dialog between the two cultures that could well be extended. In that dialog, historians, philosophers, and sociologists of science who espouse social science and objective scholarship for themselves and reject the philosophical and ideological premise of radical ontological relativism have an essential part to play.[36]

Cultural Conflict Within a Discipline: The Case of Sociology

I need to caution, now, against a possible misunderstanding. The cultural conflict we have been examining in this chapter—between science and objective scholarship on the one hand and ideology and social reform on the other—is not limited, as the examples from Snow, Gross and Levitt, and Sokal might suggest, just to a conflict between the natural sciences on one side and the humanities and social sciences on the other. There is also a good deal of conflict within the humanities

---

35. See "Sokal's Hoax: An Exchange," XLIII (1996), 54–56.
36. For an excellent sociology of science analysis of the Sokal affair as one of a class of scientific frauds, see Stephen Hilgartner, "The Sokal Affair in Context," *Science, Technology, and Human Affairs*, 22 (1997), 506–22.

and social sciences between the ideologists and those choosing the scientific and objective scholarship modes. Postmodernist, social constructivist, and feminist ideological passions in the fields of English, comparative literature, history, anthropology, and sociology—to name only some humanities and social science intellectual pursuits—are matched by a persevering and passionate commitment in these fields by scholars still striving, as they have been for a long time, for social science and objective scholarship. Each of these fields could well be a case for this discussion; I choose to limit myself to a brief treatment of the case of sociology because it is a clear case and the one with which I am most familiar.

For sociology as science and objective scholarship, we can refer to a statement I made in 1952 in "The Nature and Prospects of the Social Sciences," Chapter XI of my book *Science and The Social Order*. The statement was intended both as an analysis of the nature of social sciences, most especially, perhaps, of my own discipline, sociology, and a program for its growth and acceptance as a science on an equal footing with the natural sciences. At the time of its writing, it seemed as if such a program had a clear course ahead of it. In the event, it has had a rocky road, with many challenges from a variety of ideological movements such as the feminism, constructivism, and postmodernism I have considered earlier in this chapter. Nonetheless, it has had and still has a wide constituency among what has been, over these last forty years an ever-increasing number of sociologists. In a recent theme issue of the journal, *Sociological Forum*,[37] on the subject, *What's Wrong With Sociology?* none of the nine contributors, all veteran sociologists, took an antiscience position. Some pointed to the lack of a core scientific consensus, some deplored the politicization and ideologization of sociology, others spoke of sociologists as difficult colleagues, and some recommended that sociologists get out more and speak "to the world," but none were against a scientific sociology.[38]

---

37. Vol. 9, no. 2, 1994.

38. The *Sociological Forum* issue has now been made into a book with the same title, *What's Wrong With Sociology?* edited by Stephen Cole (Princeton, NJ: Princeton University Press, 1997). In his Introduction to the book, which now contains sixteen essays, Cole emphasizes the consensus among the contributors on the point that sociology is too much infected with ideology.

My chapter opened with a flat declaration that social science is a legitimate part of the unity of science. "Science is a unity," it said, "whatever the class of empirical materials to which it is applied, and therefore natural and social science belong together in principle." Indeed, I offered the sociological analysis of natural science that I had made in the previous ten chapters of my book as a clear example of the fact that "the social relations of science are as much subject to scientific investigation as any other class of empirical phenomena."

I asserted that human life is as impossible without some kind of social science as it is impossible without natural science. Humans have always had considerable rational commonsense knowledge of the sources and consequences of their behavior. The task for sociology and the other social sciences is to keep on making that knowledge more systematic, abstract (analytic), and comprehensive, as the natural sciences have. I pointed to the generally favorable cultural and social structural conditions for all forms of science in modern society as an asset for the development of social science. I did not, of course, fail to mention that, as there had also been in the past for the physical and biological sciences, there were powerful sources of resistance and hostility to the social sciences. I pointed to the development of new empirical research instruments and methods of analysis of the data collected by those new instruments. I suggested that the conception of an Order of Nature that Whitehead had suggested had developed in the seventeenth century needed now to be accompanied by a conception of an Order of Human Nature. In sum, in conclusion, in a statement that sprang from both scientific analysis and value commitment, I said: "It seems not unlikely that we may gradually learn that human nature is no more arbitrary, capricious, chancy, indeterminate, random, or inexplicable than physical nature or biological nature. Science in our society will not really achieve full maturity until social science comes of age with its sisters, the natural sciences." This forty-year-old statement of sociology as science is still essentially viable today.

In contrast to this statement of sociology as science, we can turn to a recent eloquent statement of sociology as ideology by Professor Charles Lemert of Wesleyan University. Lemert's statement was made in the context of a review essay[39] on five recently published volumes:

---

39. *Sociological Forum*, 11 (1996), 379–94.

the *What Is Wrong with Sociology* issue of *Sociological Forum* and four other recent and past publications, one being Edward Said's *Representations of the Intellectual*, which was discussed in chapter 2.

Lemert seems at first not to reject out-and-out scientific academic sociology, allowing at one point that that is "something it can *only partly be* (emphasis added) and, in any case, something it has tried to be only in the short time of the last three or so generations of sociology, the time of the dominance of American academic sociology." But Lemert's ambivalence[40] and concession that sociology might be partly scientific later disappears when he says "sociologists aspire to be what they may never have been capable of being, nor should have been." The ideal of scientific sociology lasted for only twenty-five years, from roughly 1940 to roughly 1965, he says, because that was a "time of postwar social change in which national political elites thought a scientific sociology might provide knowledge sufficient to the making of the good society they would lead." So, says Lemert, even when sociology thought it was being scientific, it was just being an ideology for unspecified "political elites." Such a sociology, he continues, is "at the whim of its sponsors." Many sociologists, unfortunately, still "believe received illusions about what we *were*. Those short-lived worldly successes were corrupting distractions from what I believe sociology is and should be."

Lemert declares himself a great admirer of Edward Said and his book, *Representations of the Intellectual*, and thinks sociologists should be, as Said recommends for "intellectuals," caring "amateurs," "avoiding the dulling effect of narrow specialization," and "bearing the responsibility to represent the unrepresented and unrepresentable in society." This is, says Lemert, "a call to arms," a recommendation "to resist the temptations of professionalism." As I said in my earlier discussion of Said, in chapter 2, this ideological role may be considered a noble one by many people, including some who call themselves sociologists, but it is definitely not a scientific role. Having done his or her scientific research or theory work, a sociologist might move on for a

---

40. On the matter of two cultures ambivalence, see the wise and generous dictum by John Searle, "Rationality and Realism," 82: "However, in real life people on both sides tend to be ambivalent and even confused. They are often not quite sure of what they actually think."

while to this reformer and ideological role, as many have,[41] but it can never be his or her primary scientific activity. Ideology is one essential intellectual pursuit, science is another. We need both of these intellectual pursuits, and we need a better understanding of the functions of each and of their desirable relations with one another.

---

41. As an example from my own work, see my book (with Sullivan, Makarushka, and Lally) *Research on Human Subjects: Problems of Social Control in Medical Experimentation* (New York: Russell Sage, 1973).

6

❦ ❦ ❦

The Conceptual Clarifications Made in This Book and Why They Are Important

Two major aims drive this book: rescuing the concept of culture for constructive analysis of social phenomena in general and using this improved concept to understand some key processual aspects of culture, namely, intellectual pursuits. These two aims interact and enrich each other; not only does culture, properly defined, give us a better understanding of intellectual pursuits, but the discussion of various intellectual pursuits helps to make the concept of culture clearer.

Clarification of the much-misused concept of culture advances our understanding of a number of other important sociological problems besides intellectual pursuits, although these other problems also have direct and indirect connections with intellectual pursuits. For example, when we discuss the topics of ideology and of the high-low structure of cultural systems, we illuminate important aspects of intellectual pursuits as well. Given a clear and usable theory of culture, a theory that shows its analytic difference, within the social system, both from social structure and from personality, and that emphasizes its inherently compound character, makes it possible to deal with its several components on their own terms. These components are partly independent

139

of and partly interdependent with not only the social structural and personality components of the social system but also with each other as well. Science is different from religion, values are different from philosophy, language is not the same as literature.

Using that clarified theory, further, I reveal the confusion in the use of the term "intellectual" and recommend speaking of "intellectual pursuits" rather than intellectuals. This makes it possible to deal successfully with the independence and interdependence of the several components of the compound that is culture. It makes it possible to discriminate functional types of intellectuals (or as we might more neutrally call them, "cultural experts") one from another, for example, philosophers from scientists, cultural critics (or public intellectuals, as they are now often called), from social scientists pure and simple.

Again, using this theory of culture, I can explicate the nature and functions of its several components. One such cultural component that I treat and that can be taken as a prototype of other examples, a component closely connected with much confused discussion about and by intellectuals, is ideology. I indicate how that much misused term can be defined in precise cultural terms, and how, further, it can then be used to make better analyses of a great deal of social and cultural discourse. At present, ideology is used in wildly diverse and undefined ways by public intellectuals, by social scientists, and by the man or woman in the street.

Still again, through the discussion of the general problem of the structure of culture, I clarify another specific controversial topic, a structural problem, that of whether and how useful it is to discriminate high from low culture. The analysis shows that there are essential structural and dynamic characteristics of all the idea and symbol systems that make up culture and that these characteristics result in different versions of those systems that it is indeed useful to see as hierarchical and to call high and low.

Finally, I show that it is two different sets of values—those essential, though not all-dominant components of culture—that often divide the university community into what has been called, ever since Snow's work, the two cultures and, more recently, has been called the culture wars. One group primarily values the pursuit of knowledge for its own sake. The other primarily values knowledge for its use on behalf of reformist and ideological goals. Of course, there are some in the university who make an effort to stand in both camps, at least part of the time in each, but usually members of the university community have a strong commitment one way or the other. An explicit awareness of these different, strongly held, but sometimes latent value positions may help to reduce the confusion and acrimony that often attend these culture wars that can bedevil the modern university.

Overall, it is the purpose of this book to bring to the understanding of culture in general and to the various topics related to it what I consider the superior analysis of social system theory. That general analysis and its specific applications herein are not final nor absolute. They provide grounds, as this book shows, for theoretical and empirical improvement in social analysis. For that valuable purpose I solicit the cooperation of sociologists and other social scientists. It is an important theoretical, empirical, and moral enterprise.

Index

About the Author

Bernard Barber is professor emeritus of sociology at Columbia University. He discovered the study of sociology in 1936 when he was an undergraduate at Harvard College and a student with Pitirim A. Sorokin, Robert K. Merton, Talcott Parsons, and L. J. Henderson. Ever since, for more than sixty years now, with time out only for four years of service in the United States Navy during World War II, the study of sociology has been his intellectual and moral passion and commitment. He has been author, co-author, and co-editor of fifteen books and scores of articles on many different sociological subjects, always under the guidance of social system theory. The present book builds on and advances much of his previous work.